GW00337790

A pocket book on
SLIMMING

Dr Nancy Worcester and Rhona Newman

octopus

First published 1982 by
Octopus Books Limited
59 Grosvenor Street
London W1

© **1982 Octopus Books Limited**

ISBN 0 7064 1526 4

Produced by Mandarin Publishers Ltd
22a Westlands Road, Quarry Bay, Hong Kong

Illustrations: Pru Theobalds
Diagrams: Graham Rosewarne

CONTENTS

Introduction

Isn't it amazing that we are all so thin! Weighing 340 kg (749 lb) at the age of 22 won William Campbell a place in *The Guinness Book of Records*. But a few calculations (249 kg [550 lb] 'excess fat' requires 1,925,000 Calories, divided by 8030 days of overeating) show that, in theory, Willy only overate 240 Calories a day to become so huge.

Scientists do not yet completely understand how the body manages the delicate balance between energy input (food consumption) and energy expenditure. People who stay the same weight year after year do not carefully measure their food to make certain that they are taking in precisely the right number of Calories. The body seems to have a mechanism for more or less adjusting energy output in relation to food intake.

Obesity (defined here as weighing at least 10 per cent more than you should) is a problem unique to industrialized countries as much of the third world still suffers from a lack of food. Attitudes towards body size seem to be largely determined by food availability. Plumpness is valued by societies in which it is rare. African tribes still have special fattening houses where young girls are overfed on fattening foods and allowed no physical exercise because fatness is considered beautiful. Even in wealthier countries obesity has been a status symbol until quite recently because only the rich could afford to overeat. However, all that has changed. Obesity is now the commonest nutrition problem in industrialized countries. Slimness is rarer, so more valued.

Why are we fat?

Mechanization of agriculture and the development of the food industry has meant that a more regular supply of food is available at prices most people can afford. Nutritional deficiency diseases are rare, but we can now consume too much of the wrong foods. Food supply tables comparing the 1970s to the 1910s show that 290 extra Calories are now available daily for every person.

The type of food as well as the amount has changed drastically. We are now dependent on those foods most convenient for the food industry to produce and distribute.

Our changing food habits reflect the emphasis on profitable, processed foods. More than 60 per cent of the household food budget is spent on processed foods. Wholegrain cereals and flours have been largely replaced by sugars and refined white flours which more easily lead to overconsumption. Processing often involves the addition of fat to a foodstuff and this will automatically make the food more fattening. For example, 112 g (4 oz) boiled potatoes contain 90 Calories; 112 g (4 oz) potato crisps contain 640 Calories!

Energy output has not kept up with the increase in food consumption. With modern machines, mechanical household gadgets and cars, the average person probably takes considerably less exercise than they might have done 20 or 30 years ago.

Who is fat?

Is it starting to be 'normal' to be obese? Probably at least one in four women and one in five men weigh 10 per cent more than the ideal weight in most industrial countries. In a London survey, over half of the men and women weighed were more than 15 per cent overweight.

There is some tendency for obesity to 'run in families'. A child with fat parents and siblings is more likely to become fat than is a child with thin parents and siblings. There is much controversy as to the relative importance of environmental influences (particularly the development of eating patterns) and genetic factors in this familiar tendency.

Body build, which is genetically determined, greatly influences the chances of becoming fat or the ease of avoiding it. Stout people put on weight more easily than people of a slender build.

Ironically, in contrast to days when only the rich could afford to be fat, obesity is now more common in poor people. Prevalence of obesity is about 50 per cent in social groups IV and V compared to 20 per cent in groups I, II and III. Poor people consume 28 per cent more fat and 74 per cent more sugar, but 46 per cent less vegetables and 133 per cent less fruit than do the wealthier. Workingclass men are less likely to become obese than are the women because the energy expenditure of heavy manual labour offsets the Calorie input of the less expensive diet.

In's and out's of getting fat

If energy input (food intake) is equal to energy expenditure, body weight is maintained. If someone is gaining weight, they are eating or drinking more energy (Calories) than they are using. Someone losing weight is taking in less energy than they are using (fig. 1). This seemingly simple fact becomes complex because of the numerous factors which determine how the body uses energy.

fig. 1

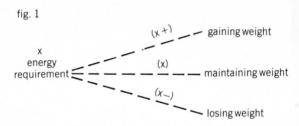

Unfortunately there is no fairness in what determines energy expenditure. Some people really can eat 5000-6000 Calories a day and maintain weight, whereas a few unlucky people can gain weight on as little as 1200 Calories a day. Recent scientific findings tell us why some people use energy efficiently, but they do not answer the question of what can be done about it.

Our attitudes towards, for example, choosing a car and living with our bodies are very different. Most of us would choose a car which efficiently uses its energy supply and can drive long distances on a little petrol. Yet those of us who enjoy food would like a body which inefficiently wastes energy so that one 'treat' after another could be 'used up' without us ever getting fat.

Regardless of energy requirements, fig. 1 holds true for everyone. If your energy requirement (x) is 5000 Calories, you will maintain weight on that amount; you will gradually gain on 5200 (x+) Calories or lose on 4800 (x−) Calories. If you are only using up 1200 Calories a day, you will gain weight on as little as 1300 Calories and you will need to take less than 1200 Calories to lose.

Table 1	Estimated Average Daily Energy Requirements		Calories
Males	18-34	sedentary	2700
		moderately active	3000
		very active	3600
	35-64	sedentary	2600
		moderately active	2900
		very active	3600
	65-74		2350
Females	18-54	most occupations	2200
		very active	2500
	55-74		2050

Department of Health and Social Security

Energy requirements vary greatly from one individual to another and will differ in the same individual when that person is more or less active than usual. Recommended intake of nutrient tables give an energy figure which represents the *average* requirement for each *group* of people. Therefore about half the individuals in each group will require more energy than suggested and half will require less. If you are maintaining your weight, you should be able to calculate your own energy requirements by carefully recording everything you eat for a period of time (three to four weeks) and calculating your average intake.

Getting fat vs. staying fat
Anyone with a weight problem has at one time eaten more than their Calorie requirement in order to have gained weight. However, you do not need to 'overeat' to remain fat. In fact, overweight people often eat less than people who do not have a weight problem (page 12):

Gaining weight can be harder than losing it
Very little attention is focused on the person who wants to, or needs to, gain weight. A person who naturally burns off Calories easily will need to consume enormous quantities of rich foods in order to gain 1 kg (2.2 lb). Such a diet can be expensive, anti-social and difficult to consume.

Input: food is fattening
The energy value of food is measured in Calories. The

7

nutritionists' unit, the Calories (kilocalorie), is written with a capital C so that it is not confused with the physicists' calorie which is 1000 times smaller. The metric form of Calorie counting is joule counting. One Calorie equals 4.2 kilojoules (kJ); 1000 Calories equals 4200 kilojoules or 4.2 megajoules (MJ).

As Calories are simply a way of measuring energy, Calories and energy are synonymous. People often wrongly attach totally different connotations to the two words implying 'energy is good for the body' but 'Calories are fattening'. Sugar and soft drink manufacturers use 'full of energy' as a selling point, but they would never consider advertising 'full of Calories'.

Table 2   Energy Value of Pure Nutrients

	Calories/g	Calories/oz	kJ/g
Vitamins	0	0	0
Minerals	0	0	0
Water	0	0	0
Carbohydrates	3.75	106	16
Proteins	4.00	114	17
Fats	9.00	256	37
Alcohol	7.00	199	29

Most foods are mixtures of several nutrients and the energy value of the food will be determined by the relative proportions of those nutrients (Table 2). Because fat is a particularly concentrated source of energy (256 Calories to 28 g [1 oz]), foods which contain a lot of fat are always more fattening than foods with little or no fat. The high fat content of cheddar cheese compared to cottage cheese means that cheddar contains nearly four times as many Calories. Although water, vitamins and minerals are essential for body functioning, these nutrients do not give the body energy. Fresh fruits and vegetables, usually rich sources of vitamins and minerals, contain as much as 96 per cent water and no fat, so are ideal low-Calorie foods.

Nutritionists have a special instrument, the bomb calorimeter, for determining the energy value of food. Sometimes Calorie tables give slightly different values for the same food. This variation is mostly explained by 'sampling differences' — no two bananas, for example, are exactly the same. The small variation from one table to another is insignificant in calculating total Calorie intake for a day.

Fat, because it holds energy in a compact form, is useful in reducing the bulk of the diet. The Chinese diet is low in fat so more than 450 g (1 lb) of rice a day must be consumed to meet the body's energy needs. Westerners living in China have great difficulty learning to eat this

		g	oz
Table 3	Lard	11	0.4
100 Calorie	Butter	13	0.5
(418 kJ)	Peanuts	17	0.6
Portions	Sweet biscuits	17	0.6
of Food	Milk chocolate	17	0.6
	Chocolate cake	20	0.7
	Potato crisps	20	0.7
	Bacon, back, cooked	22	0.8
	Double cream	22	0.8
	Cheddar cheese	25	0.9
	Sugar	25	0.9
	Cornflakes	27	1.0
	Pork sausage, fried	31	1.1
	Roast pork	32	1.1
	Beef steak, grilled	33	1.2
	Marmalade	38	1.3
	Currants, dried	41	1.4
	Bread	41	1.4
	Potatoes, chips, fried	42	1.5
	Herring, fried	43	1.5
	Ice cream, vanilla	52	1.8
	Eggs	61	2.1
	Chicken, roast	68	2.4
	Cottage cheese	88	3.1
	Baked beans	107	3.8
	Steamed cod	122	4.3
	Potatoes old, boiled	130	4.6
	Bananas	130	4.6
	Milk, whole	151	¼ pint
	Yogurt, low fat, natural	190	6.7
	Peas, boiled	204	7.2
	Apples	213	7.5
	Oranges	286	10.1
	Tomatoes	715	25.2

quantity of food. Because Western diets are so high in fat (40-45 per cent of Calories come from fat), a relatively small quantity of food can provide many Calories and it is easy to take in more Calories than the body requires.

From the list of foods in Table 3 choose several which you consume regularly. First, without weighing foods, try to prepare 100 Calorie portions of the foods. Then, by accurately weighing the food, evaluate how accurate you were at estimating the energy value of foods. This 100 Calorie portion would represent one tenth of a 1000 Calorie diet!

Output: using up energy
Energy is used by the body both for those functions over which we have no control (basic metabolism) and for those activities which we do control (sitting, standing, exercising). Additionally, some of the energy supplied to the body from food is inefficiently 'wasted' as heat.

BMR – something you have to live with
Approximately two thirds of our energy intake is used for those involuntary activities (brain functioning, regulation of heart beat, breathing, maintenance of body temperature, transmission of nerve impulses) essential for life and proper body functioning. The amount needed for these activities can be measured in people at complete rest and is called the *basal metabolic rate* (BMR). BMR varies from one person to another, ranging from 1200-1800 Calories per day. The following factors affect BMR:

1. *Body surface area.* Bigger people need more energy than smaller people. A tall thin person has more body surface than a short fat person.

2. *Age.* BMR decreases with age (after age two years).

3. *Sex.* Women have a lower BMR than men.

4. *Body temperature.* BMR goes up by 13 per cent when body temperature rises by $1°$ C $(1.8°$ F).

5. *External temperature.* BMR can rise in low temperatures to help maintain body temperature.

6. *Growing processes.* BMR rises during periods of growth and pregnancy.

7. *Muscular work.* BMR can be increased by muscular work.

8. *Hormones.* BMR can be influenced by hormonal

changes. Excess secretion of thyroxine or adrenalin causes BMR to rise.

BMR is something you have to live with as trying to change it can be dangerous. However, there are ways to take advantage of natural changes in BMR. Having a fever will cause BMR to rise. Most people 'accidentally' lose weight when they are ill but return to old eating patterns and gain weight as soon as they are well. This could be an ideal time to change eating patterns and keep off those lost kilograms.

The underrated importance of exercise

The role of exercise in weight control is often underemphasized. It is easy to understand this attitude when you look at an exercise table (page 12) and see that it would take more than one hour of walking to 'work off' one chocolate bar. However, unless you give up the chocolate bar how else can you 'burn off' the extra 310 Calories?

Exercise has an invaluable role to play in preventing weight gain (pages 48–57), although both exercise and dietary restriction may be required for weight loss. Regular exercise tunes up the body so that it runs at its best, ironically 'wasting' maximum energy. BMR is increased by exercise, particularly after a meal, and exercise increases the ratio of muscle to fat.

Obesity is rare in those whose lives involve regular physical activity (heavy manual labourers, athletes, professional dancers). People often claim that they never had a weight problem until they stopped having regular physical activity. Studies show that 'obese' are considerably less active than 'non-obese' but these studies do not clarify whether the lack of activity led to the obesity or whether being fat made them feel less inclined to exercise.

Exercise is a very personal matter. To incorporate regular exercise into your life, you must find a form which suits you and your lifestyle. At the very least walking up and down stairs for ten minutes a day could keep off 4.5 kg (10 lb) a year.

Anyone starting on a routine of regular exercise should not be concerned by an initial increase in appetite. This will not be a problem once an exercise pattern is established. In most people, exercise improves appetite control.

Table 4 Approximate Energy Requirement for Certain Physical Activities	
Activity	Approximate Calories per hour
Billiards, sailing, golf, cricket, gardening	180-200
Strolling, dancing, surfing, gentle rowing, lawn mowing	280
Walking at average pace, cycling, badminton, fencing, rambling, basketball	360
Jogging, tennis, climbing, swimming, skiing, woodchopping	440
Sprinting, boxing, squash, rowing (sculls), bicycling (fast)	600-700

The fat get fatter

Losing weight *is* possible, but no sensible person would say that it is easy. It is easier to keep off extra weight than to take off extra weight. And most unfairly, a slim person can lose weight more easily than can an obese person.

The body's metabolism (the way it uses food and energy) adapts to the state of being fat in such a way as to perpetuate the condition. Obese can be very efficient at using the energy from food and seem to have lost the ability to waste energy. Obese expend less energy performing an activity (walking, climbing, etc.) than non-obese and because obese tend to take less exercise, they benefit less from the metabolic advantages of exercise. A thick layer of fat insulates an obese person from adjusting BMR to cold temperatures.

The metabolic changes associated with obesity tend to be reversed by weight loss, proving that they are adaptations to fatness. On the other hand, a very few individuals seem to have metabolic problems which predispose them to obesity. Most of these people have been obese since childhood and have great difficulty losing weight even in clinical situations. 'Metabolic obesity' is currently the topic of much scientific research.

Health implications of fatness

For thousands of years, the body's ability to store fat was a life-saving phenomenon. With an erratic food supply, fat stored in the body aided survival through lean periods. Today's overweight people would have been another generation's survivors. The body's ability to store fat has now been changed from a life-saving mechanism to a health hazard.

The woman who cannot fit into her tight jeans does not have a health problem — she has just gained a few extra kilograms and is worried about her appearance. A person who is excessively fat has a health risk which is reversed by a loss of weight.

People who lose weight for health reasons seem to be more successful at losing weight than those who try to lose to improve their appearance. Hopefully understanding the health risks of fatness will be a useful incentive to someone who has already decided to lose weight.

Living with fat

It is hard work for the body to carry around extra weight. Try attaching a 4.5 kg (10 lb) bag of potatoes to yourself and carry it around for several hours as you walk up stairs and do the cooking and cleaning. Compare how you normally feel when doing these activities to how you feel when you are carrying the extra load.

Complications can arise when the body tries to carry around more weight than it can comfortably support. The human skeleton does not get bigger or stronger to adapt, so flat feet, backache and arthritis are common side-effects of obesity. Fat around the chest can interfere with breathing and cause shortness of breath. Abdominal hernias, varicose veins and high blood pressure are also problems commonly associated with being overweight.

Everyday happenings can be more dangerous and traumatic for the overweight person. Accidents are more common both at home and at work because a heavy person tends to move more slowly. Doctors often ask patients to lose weight before an operation as simple surgery becomes more risky when performed on an overweight person. It is easy to imagine the problems of going through masses of fat to find a small organ or blood vessel. Also, anaesthesia is

13

more hazardous as anaesthetics are fat soluble so it is difficult to determine the correct dosage. Pregnancy also can be more complicated for an overweight woman (page 41).

fig. 2 **Excess mortality among overweight men and women (aged 15-69) by cause.**

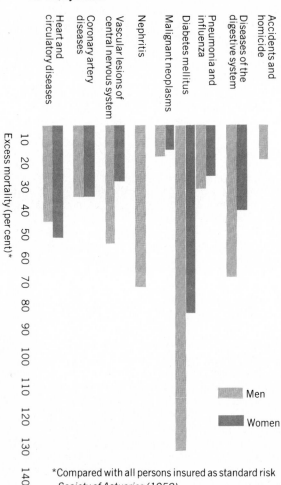

*Compared with all persons insured as standard risk
Society of Actuaries (1959)

Dying with fat

Your chances of living a long healthy life are much slimmer if you are obese. Mortality figures for obese compared to non-obese are particularly striking for the young and middle-aged. Surplus weight has been incriminated as a health hazard related to a wide variety of diseases (fig. 2).

Increased death risk is directly related to the degree of obesity (fig. 3). The dangers of obesity are reversible with weight loss. Fig. 3 shows that even a small weight loss can improve health risks.

fig. 3 **Excess mortality among overweight men and women (aged 15-69).**

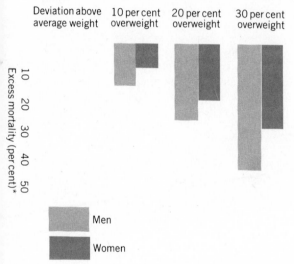

*Compared with all persons insured as standard risks
Society of Actuaries (1959)

Health problems can make you fat

Any health problem — physical or visual handicap, being bedridden, mental depression — which interferes with the body's ability to expend energy in the form of exercise in relation to food consumption, can eventually lead to obesity.

15

Psychological implications of fatness

The nutritional needs of the body could be supplied with a properly balanced chemical solution, yet we would be horrified if this were all we could consume or all that we had to offer to our friends and families. Most slimmers have read numerous books on nutrition and slimming, and understand the scientific concepts involved and yet still cannot lose weight. Why? Food is absolutely central to our lives but the social and psychological reasons for, and consequences of, food choices are only starting to be examined.

Despite the fact that obesity is becoming increasingly common in our society and must be considered a social problem, obese individuals suffer severe prejudice simply because of their physique. Studies consistently show that the obese physique is more strongly stereotyped than any other physique, and undesirable and unpopular traits are commonly associated with this group. These prejudices are held by well and lesser educated groups alike and the negative stereotyping of obesity appears to be strong even by the age of six. Obese people themselves exhibit an unfavourable attitude towards the obese. Unlike other weight groups which attribute negative characteristics to both extremely thin and extremely overweight shapes, the obese group positively stereotypes (idealizes) the extremely thin physique.

Negative stereotyping is *not* based on reality, but obese individuals suffer real disadvantages because of this prejudice. Job agencies admit that it is more difficult for an overweight person to get a job. Applicants with identical IQ's are much less likely to get a university place if they are obese than if they are of average weight. Slimmers who have successfully lost a lot of weight are often appalled at how much easier it is 'to be liked' as a thin person when they feel they were just as likeable when overweight. Clothes could be an important way to counteract the negative stereotype of obesity, but the limited range of clothes available in large sizes only helps reinforce the negative images.

The prejudices exhibited towards obesity will of course affect how overweight people see themselves. Adolescents are particularly apt to suffer from a disturbed body image.

Being obese during adolescence can lead to attitude changes quite different from those exhibited by people who become obese later in life. Obese adolescent girls can show traits (passivity, withdrawal, acute sensitivity) similar to those of other minority groups who may be subjected to intense prejudice.

'Fat people are jolly'

An overweight person is often depicted as an easy going clown who is always fun to have around. Since overweight people tend to move more slowly they can simply appear less tense. The roundness of the overweight person may appear more warm and cuddly than the angularity of a thin person. The obese person may adopt a jolly personality to cover up the problems of being overweight or to subconsciously play along with the feeling that overweight people are not taken seriously. Or, excess body weight may be a result of the way certain personality types use food in their lives.

Extroverts and introverts respond to food in different ways. Introverts tend to have more food dislikes, eat at regular times and are more satisfied on a restricted diet. In contrast, extroverts respond to external stimuli (attractive food, social situations, set meal times) so may eat when they are not actually hungry. Extroverts like a great variety of foods and have fewer dislikes. From this generalization, it is easy to see that a jolly extrovert could easily grow into a fat jolly person.

The incidence of suicide is only three-quarters as high in the obese as it is in the general population and the obese, as a group, suffer from anxiety and depression less than do their normal weight peers. Obese individuals may be able to use food and overeating as a way to relieve stress and tension in their lives and many have been conditioned, since early childhood, to use food as a reward. The obese are likely to turn to food at a time of stress whereas many people feel less hungry and lose weight during these periods.

Generalizations are dangerous when applied to individuals. However, some people are extremely unhappy because of their excess weight and may be aware of suffering the real disadvantages discussed above.

Women and slimming

Women are seen as the providers of food and are expected to nourish the men and children in their lives even in the most difficult circumstances. Responsibility for food preparation imposes constant deadlines on a woman's life. Several hours a day may be taken up with food preparation and shopping. Food advertising, which reinforces stereotypes, is aimed at women trying to convince each one that their special product will help her fulfil her role as superwoman.

But even superwoman will start to feel the contradiction when she realizes she is also supposed to stay slim while lovingly preparing all these creative dishes. Ideally, of course, she will make staying slim appear perfectly natural so that no one else is aware that she has to watch her weight.

Plumpness is common, so slimness is valued. But somehow the plump woman is made to feel a misfit. Women are judged by their appearance far more than men. Consequently, women are much more concerned about their weight than men. Overweight women are very aware of being overweight and many have tried to lose weight whereas more than 30 per cent of overweight men are unaware of being overweight and many obese men do not try to lose weight. More than a third of suitable weight women feel they weigh too much and many have tried to lose. Such a tendency does not exist in average weight men.

Some women eat compulsively even though they would like to be thin. Many women who know how to lose weight do not lose weight or quickly put on any weight which is lost. Is it possible that some women overeat because subconsciously they want to be fat? Are some women afraid of the expectations which society would place upon them as thin people and, subconsciously, do they sense that their fatness protects them from these expectations? Why women eat compulsively and why women do or do not lose weight are complex psychological issues which women themselves are starting to explore. (*Fat is A Feminist Issue*, Susie Orbach, Paddington Press, London, 1978.)

The emphasis on female slimness starts early and is exaggerated during adolescence. Girls learn early to think there is something wrong with their bodies if they are not the same as the slim, bosomy model. Over 80 per cent of adolescent girls want to lose weight but less than 20 per cent of adolescent boys are concerned about this. Most frightening, nearly 60 per cent of 'thin' adolescent girls want to lose weight.

Anorexia nervosa

Anorexia nervosa is the extreme overreaction to the pressure to slim. The anorexic, usually a young woman aged between 14 and 23, becomes obsessed with food so stops eating and perceives herself as overweight even when she is considerably underweight.

Rejecting food is an indirect way of rejecting growing up as a woman and the conflicting expectations of what that role means in this society. For the young woman who feels she has no control over the changes happening in her body and her life, rejecting food may be a desperate attempt to take some control.

Psychological problems of slimming

Too often overweight people assume they should slim and feel guilty if they are not slimming. If you are not going to work at slimming, it will be better to make a conscious decision not to slim and work at liking the body the way it is. If you decide to try slimming, you should be aware of the consequences of success or failure at this venture. Dieting will probably make you more aware of food than usual. To have to cut down on food at exactly the time you become obsessed with it will be very trying.

If you have great difficulty in losing weight, you may feel that this represents a failure to take control of your life. A slimming support group may be particularly useful in this situation.

The unpleasantness of being overweight may cause certain anxieties in an individual which could be diminished by weight reduction. On the other hand, if the obese person has been able to use eating as a means of relieving anxieties, food restriction could remove this outlet and increase tension. Of course, a person who has been overweight and manages to lose weight quite quickly may feel disorientated suddenly living in a thin body. They may miss not being able to blame their problems on being fat.

19

When do people get fat?
Any situation which causes you to eat more, exercise less or changes your metabolism, can lead to weight increase. Any change in lifestyle (living with someone, living alone, having children) may influence these factors.

Fat children tend to become fat adults (page 43). Approximately one third of obese adults were overweight as children.

People tend to put on weight as they get older although there is no reason to think this is natural or healthy. Energy requirements decrease with age. An average woman requires 150 Calories less per day at 55 than she did at 35. But few people cut down on Calories once food patterns are established. Lifestyle and responsibilities later in life may include less exercise and more social eating and drinking, or at least more money to buy more food.

Smoking: Both food intake and metabolic rate seem to be influenced by smoking. You are likely to gain weight while you are trying to give up smoking unless you make a conscious decision to control food intake and increase exercise at this time.

Hormonal changes: These can affect the way the body uses food. When hormonal changes occur, many individuals find that they gain weight more easily than before. In *adolescence* both girls and boys experience huge hormonal changes in their bodies. Female hormones particularly increase the build up of fat at this time. Therefore it is important to establish good eating and exercise patterns.

Contraceptive pills contain female hormones so they too cause hormonal changes in the body. Many women gain some weight on the pill because of fluid retention (the kidneys excrete less than usual) and because the hormones in the pill (oestrogen and progesterone) build up tissues and in some cases cause fat to be laid down in the body more easily. A woman who is particularly sensitive to these changes may be happier on a different brand of contraceptive pill or with another form of contraceptive.

Pregnancy: (See page 41).

Women often start gaining weight in their late 40s and 50s due to the hormonal changes of *menopause*, reduced energy requirements of this age and changes in responsibilities (children leaving home, etc.).

How to tell if you are too fat

An image of the ideal body is sold to us by the media along with the clothes, the cosmetics, or the lifestyle. But clothes that look good on a model are a size too small to move in and people in this profession usually have a 'weight contract' which stipulates how little he or she must weigh in order to keep the job.

If we were not given such impossible expectations to live up to, we would be more realistic in judging whether we are too fat. Everytime we run for a bus or try to wear clothes we bought five years ago we have a realistic reminder of whether we need to lose weight.

The health risks involved in being overweight are associated with the build up of excess fat. It is possible, although not common except in athletes, to weigh more than average because of well-developed muscles. A doctor can determine whether you are overweight because of fat or muscle by measuring skinfold thickness with special calipers. Most of us do not need sophisticated methods to determine whether we are too fat.

The 'pinch test' can be used to mimic the doctor's skinfold thickness test. Using your thumb and first finger pinch at extra flesh wherever you tend to put on fat — waist, midriff, underarm. If you can get hold of more than 2.5 cm (1 in), you are probably carrying around extra fat.

Ideal weight is a very individual matter. You may be able to determine your ideal weight by recollecting your weight at the stage of your (adult) life when you felt your best. If you are as thin and fit as ever, your weight is probably not adversely affecting your health. If you are heavier than you were at another stage, you are probably gradually accumulating extra fat. (This method is not suitable for someone who has always been 'fat'.)

Life insurance companies have compiled both average weight tables and ideal weight tables on the basis of the volumes of information which they have about people's weight and its relationship to life expectancy.

Ideal (or desirable) weight tables show the best weight in relation to height for optimum life expectancy. Average weight tables simply show the average of the actual weights recorded. Average weights are considerably higher than ideal weights and are getting steadily heavier every decade, showing that the population as a whole is heavier than desirable and is getting heavier. Average weights are now approximately 6-11 kg (15-25 lb) heavier than ideal weights (Table 5).

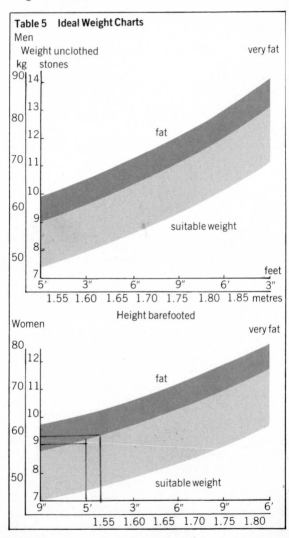

Table 5 Ideal Weight Charts

Sensible slimming

The ideal diet should be a subtle variation of the regular diet which simply encourages weight loss rather than weight gain or maintenance. But few people can choose a sensible slimming diet because most of us are unaware of what our unique, personal, normal diet is. For many people there is a period of time between making the decision to slim and starting the process of slimming. Using this time to study regular eating patterns can be an excellent investment for long-term successful slimming.

Before slimming, spend a couple of weeks recording everything you eat and drink. Record accurate quantities of the foods consumed. Try to note the time of day and the circumstances (after lunch, cleaning up left-overs; evening meal with friends; reward for house cleaning; feeling depressed). Eat as normally as possible so that your eating habits are not influenced by your record keeping.

After a couple of weeks, take a careful look at the pattern which has emerged. What percentage of your food is taken as 'proper meals' versus snacks? What factors influence what you eat and when you eat? After having kept your record, try to add up your total Calorie intake for several typical days to figure your average Calorie intake.

Having established your normal pattern, this can now be altered slightly to reduce Calorie intake. The more closely a slimming diet resembles your normal diet and fits into your lifestyle, the more likely you are to stick with it. If your average Calorie intake is quite high, you may not need to do anything very drastic to lose weight. On the other hand, if your Calorie intake is already low, you may need to be quite strict with yourself in order to lose weight.

Identify the 'empty Calories' (page 24) in your diet and see where these can be eliminated, portions cut in half, or where other foods and beverages could be substituted. Make it a priority to reduce your sweet tooth even if you cannot give up sugar. Discover where fat sneaks into your diet and start to reduce it. Use less butter, margarine and oil. Choose low-fat methods of cooking (eat potatoes baked instead of fried) and low-fat versions (cottage or curd cheese instead of cheddar). Plan your snacks (page 36) and make yourself see them as a part of your total intake.

Value for calories

Spending Calories on a slimming diet is like spending pennies on a budget. When money is abundant, you can waste money on luxuries and there will still be money left for essentials. If you overeat a variety of foods, the essential nutrients will probably be supplied along with the over-abundance of Calories. If you simply cut portions in half, you would not only halve the number of Calories but would also halve the amount of nutrients.

A slimmer must budget Calories to find the best nutritional bargains. One hundred Calories spent on sugar makes no contribution to the nutritional requirement but 100 Calories spent on cottage cheese contributes protein, calcium and other nutrients. All the needs of the body can be fulfilled easily on a 1000 Calorie diet if suitable foods are chosen, but the body could develop an overdraft if 1000 Calories were wasted on empty Calories.

Empty calories

Foods and beverages which contribute very little nutritive value in relation to their high Calorie content are considered empty Calories. These are strictly luxury goods on a slimming diet. The successful slimmer minimizes or eliminates empty Calorie foods (sweets, crisps, high-calorie sweet drinks) from the diet. Although many foods (vinegar, grapefruit, eggs) have been wrongly labelled as having special slimming properties, there is no such thing as a special food which helps to take off fat.

What is a diet?

The term diet simply refers to a pattern of eating. But it is often misused to refer to a pattern of eating for weight reduction. These special patterns of eating should be referred to as slimming diets.

Nutrition and slimming

The diet must supply the body with plenty of the specific nutrients which it needs to survive and function. But we do not consciously decide to have 5 g of protein and 40 mg of vitamin C when we reach for our toast and orange juice. We choose the foods rather than the nutrients we wish to consume, so it is useful to have a guide to which foods will supply the essential nutrients.

Food group evaluation of nutrition

Foods can be divided into food groups on the basis of the similarity of their nutrient content. The four food groups and the nutrients contributed by each group to the average (British) diet are summarized in Table 6.

Table 6   Percentage Contribution of Food Groups to the Nutrient Content of the Average Diet (U.K.)

Milk Group
Energy = 15%
Protein = 25%
Calcium = 62%
Vitamin A = 19%
Thiamin = 15%
Riboflavin = 40%
Nicotinic Acid = 15%
Vitamin D = 14%

Bread and Cereal Group
Energy = 29%
Protein = 26%
Calcium = 22%
Iron = 32%
Thiamin = 43%
Riboflavin = 15%
Nicotinic Acid = 21%

Fruit and Vegetable Group
Energy = 10%
Protein = 10%
Iron = 23%
Vitamin A = 24% (from veg)
Thiamin = 20% (mostly from veg)
Riboflavin = 10% (mostly from veg)
Nicotinic Acid = 16% (mostly from veg)
Vitamin C = 86%

Meat Group
Energy = 19%
Protein = 37%
Iron = 35%
Vitamin A = 28%
Thiamin = 20%
Riboflavin = 28%
Nicotinic Acid = 41%
Vitamin D = 36% (from fish and eggs)

HMSO Manual of Nutrition

The milk group, including all dairy products and cheese, is valued for its protein, calcium, and riboflavin contribution to the diet. The meat, fish and egg group contributes protein, iron and vitamins. The fruits and vegetables are important for their vitamin content, but specific foods make very different contributions to the diet. Citrus fruits are excellent sources of vitamin C. Dark green and yellow vegetables are major sources of vitamin A. The importance of the bread and cereal group in supplying protein, minerals and vitamins is too often forgotten or undervalued. In addition to 'natural' nutrients in the grains, many governments require that bread and cereal products are enriched with vitamins (B) and minerals (iron and calcium) so as to improve the nutritional status of the community.

Fats and oils, sugars and sweets, are not emphasized in a food group evaluation of nutrition. Although some items in these groups provide essential nutrients, these foods are usually plentiful in most diets and may need to be discouraged, not encouraged.

A daily mixture of servings from each food group will ensure an adequate intake of nutrients. A slimmer will want to choose low-fat, low-sugar versions of their choices.

It is important to note that Table 6 merely summarizes the actual contribution which food groups make to the nutrient content of the diet for the population (British) as a whole. In no way should this pattern be considered as the best. There are hundreds of healthy variations. The contribution which different foods and food groups make to the diet varies enormously from one individual to another and from one country to another.

With careful thought and nutritional knowledge, it is of course possible to plan an adequate diet without a major contribution from one or more groups. The low-carbohydrate diet minimizes the contribution of the bread and cereal group. Vegetarian and vegan diets eliminate meat, and sometimes milk, and the dieter needs to be certain that the nutrients usually supplied from these foods are provided by other foods.

The diet must supply protein, carbohydrate, fat, vitamins, minerals and water to the body. A slimming diet must be a nutrient-concentrated diet while supplying only a minimum number of Calories.

Proteins — overemphasized?

Dietary proteins are essential for supplying the amino acids (sub-units of protein) required for growth and maintenance of body tissue. The amino acids can only be supplied by protein in the diet. In a situation where the diet does not supply sufficient fat or carbohydrate, protein can be used to take care of the energy-giving roles of these nutrients, but if the diet does not supply enough protein there is no way in which carbohydrates or fats can fulfil the specific requirements for amino acids.

Proteins are extremely important, but too often common nutritional knowledge begins and ends with this fact. The average Westerner consumes at least twice as much protein as is needed. There is no biological advantage to consuming more protein than the body requires. Extra protein is used as an energy source which is just as fattening as carbohydrates. As proteins tend to be relatively expensive, it is an expensive way to get fat.

Meat, fish, eggs and milk are excellent protein sources, but they are erroneously overemphasized as the only sources. Wheat contains 10 per cent protein and the bread and cereal group contributes more than a quarter of the protein to the average diet. Cereal and vegetable products can be the major source of protein in inexpensive diets. Dried skim milk is an excellent, inexpensive source of protein containing 35 per cent protein by weight compared to beef which contains 18 per cent protein.

At one time it was believed that a high-protein diet could speed up metabolism, but this is now known not to be the case. There is also a belief that an expensive high-protein diet is essential for slimming. A slimming diet need not be either high protein or expensive. The body holds slightly less water on a high-protein diet so slimmers can experience immediate weight loss on a high protein diet simply because of water loss.

For the best nutrient to Calorie value, a slimmer will want to choose low-fat foods as protein sources, and prepare these with a minimum of fat. Table 7 summarizes the protein content of 100 Calorie portions of some good protein sources and shows that you do not need to consume a high Calorie diet to provide the body with essential protein (about 40 g [1.4 oz] a day).

Table 7 Protein Content of 100 Calorie Portions of Food	Food (100 Calorie)	Protein (g)
	Double cream (0.8 oz)	0.4
	Potato crisps (0.7 oz)	1.16
	Single cream (1.9 oz)	1.48
	Rice (1 oz raw)	1.73
	Spaghetti (1 oz raw)	2.72
	Potatoes (4.6 oz raw)	2.76
	Pork sausage (1 oz)	2.89
	Bread, white (1.4 oz)	3.18
	Bread, wholemeal (1.5 oz)	3.98
	Steak & kidney pie (1.2 oz)	4.37
	Peanuts (0.6 oz)	4.79
	Milk, whole (5.4 fl oz)	5.08
	Bacon (0.8 oz cooked)	5.48
	Cheddar cheese (0.9 oz)	6.16
	Fish fingers (2 oz)	7.08
	Herring (1.5 oz)	7.18
	Beef (1.6 oz)	8.00
	Lentils (1.2 oz raw)	8.07
	Haricot beans (1.4 oz raw)	8.36
	Eggs (1 large)	8.37
	Yogurt, low-fat (6.7 oz)	9.43
	Liver (1.4 oz fried)	10.20
	Peas (7.2 oz boiled)	10.20
	Skim milk (1 oz dried)	10.23
	Broad beans (5.1 oz raw)	10.43
	Cottage cheese (3.1 oz)	13.40
	Chicken (2.4 oz roast)	16.76
1 oz = 28.35 g	White fish (4.6 oz)	22.90

Animal vs. vegetable proteins

Twenty-two amino acids occur in protein. A single protein is made up of several hundred of these amino acids joined together in a specific arrangement. The body can change some amino acids into other amino acids, but eight essential amino acids cannot be made in the body so must be supplied by the diet.

These essential amino acids need to be provided by the diet in a ratio similar to the ratio in which the body uses them. The amino acid pattern of most animal foods is more similar to the ratio the body needs than is the pattern of most plant foods. However, this difference between animal and plant foods is only important if a food is eaten in isolation. Once plant foods are mixed, the deficient amino acid in one plant food can be balanced by an excess of that amino acid in another plant food.

In general, animal products and legumes (pulses) are low in one amino acid and cereals are low in another. Combinations of legumes or animal products plus cereals give an excellent amino acid pattern (beans on toast, macaroni and cheese, milk on cereals).

Carbohydrates are not what they used to be

The amount of carbohydrate consumed per person has not changed much in the last 200 years, but the type of carbohydrate has changed drastically. Carbohydrates now tend to be more refined and starches have been replaced by sugars. The average sugar consumption is now 1 kg (2.2 lb) per week, 25 times more than in the early 1800s. Although we are aware of adding sugar to our diet, two-thirds to three-quarters of the sugar sneaks into our diets unnoticed in both sweet and savoury manufactured foods.

Sugar rapidly gets into the bloodstream and gives you a lift, but it merely speeds up and exaggerates the raised blood glucose levels and insulin response which occur after a meal of mixed foods. The quick sugar lift may be followed an hour or two later by a feeling of hunger and lack of energy. Sugar can easily convince the body that it needs more energy than it actually requires.

The replacement of starch by sugar is not a healthy change in our diet. High sugar consumption is certainly a factor in the prevalence of obesity and dental caries. It may also be related to the increased prevalence of heart disease and diabetes.

Calorie content and sweetness of carbohydrate should not be confused. All pure carbohydrates contain 3.75 Calories per gram regardless of their sweetness, but some sugars are much sweeter than others. Sucrose (table sugar) tastes six times sweeter than lactose, the sugar in milk. Glucose tastes three-quarters as sweet as sucrose. Fructose (fruit sugar) tastes nearly twice (1.7 times) as sweet as sucrose.

Carbohydrates tend to be cheap, easy to store sources of energy. As such, they have an important role to play in the diet of poor people. If carbohydrates and fats can fulfil all the energy requirements of the body, no expensive protein needs to be wasted for energy and can be saved for specific 'protein' jobs.

Approximately 50 per cent of Calories in the average (Western) diet come from carbohydrates. To reduce energy intake a slimmer can cut down on carbohydrates. Sources of carbohydrates which carry other nutrients should be consumed in place of empty Calorie foods. Brown sugars and honeys must be considered as empty Calories in the same way as refined white sugar and sugar products. Ideally, whole grain cereals and breads should be encouraged.

Fibre and roughage

Fibre can be a healthy, satisfying part of a slimming diet. Fibre contributes bulk and helps create a feeling of fullness. The body cannot digest the fibre part of food. Thus, fibre goes in and out of the body without being absorbed so the body can take no energy (Calories) from it.

Food moves through the system more rapidly on a high-fibre diet. Fibre holds water as it goes through the system so that high-fibre diets form soft, bulky bowel movements in contrast to the small hard stools on a low-fibre diet.

The main dietary source of fibre are cereals and flours made from whole grains, fruits and vegetables, seeds and nuts. Although the actual fibre part of a foodstuff contains no Calories, high-fibre foods are not necessarily low-Calorie foods.

Fats – full of energy

The fats are extremely concentrated sources of energy providing more than twice as many Calories per gram as either proteins or carbohydrates. In contrast to poorer countries where fat accounts for 15 per cent of total energy, more than 40 per cent of Calories in Western diets are derived from fat. Only one-third of the fat in our diet is consumed as visible fat – butter, margarine, cooking oils. It is easy to be unaware of the large quantities of fat (about 80 grams a day) taken in meat, milk, eggs, cakes and biscuits.

A very small quantity of fat is required in the diet to provide the essential fatty acids and to carry fat soluble vitamins (A,D,E,K). Little is known about essential fatty acid requirements in humans because even the poorest diets supply sufficient quantities.

However, there is much controversy about the amount of fat to consume and also the type of fat to consume. Some epidemiological studies show a correlation between saturated fat intake and the incidence of heart disease. There is evidence to suggest that blood cholesterol levels are lower, at least in the short term, on a polyunsaturated fat diet. For prevention of heart disease, it is often recommended that total fat intake should be decreased and there should be some replacement of saturated fats with polyunsaturated fats. The body is capable of making cholesterol, so it is questionable whether dietary cholesterol should be minimized to lower blood cholesterol levels. If animal fats (meat, eggs, milk, butter) in the diet are partially replaced

GUIDE TO FATS

Most foods contain a mixture of different types of fat.

All fats (regardless of type) provide 9 Cal/g (256 Cal/oz).

Polyunsaturated fats
Vegetable sources (including grains) usually contain a high ratio of polyunsaturated to saturated fatty acids.

A food containing a high proportion of polyunsaturated fatty acids will be liquid (oil) at room temperature (corn oil is high in polyunsaturated fat).

Saturated fats
Animal sources usually contain a high ratio of saturated to polyunsaturated fatty acids.

A food containing a high proportion of saturated fatty acids will be solid (hard) at room temperature (lard is high in saturated fat).

Unsaturated fats can be turned into saturated fats by a hydrogenation process (as in the manufacture of margarine).

Cholesterol
Cholesterol is found only in foods of animal origin. The body can make its own cholesterol.

by vegetable fats (vegetable oils, margarine, grains and vegetables), the intake of both dietary cholesterol and saturated fat will be lower.

Directly, or indirectly, a slimming diet will need to reduce fat consumption in order to reduce Calorie intake. Fats contribute to the taste and texture of meals so some thought needs to be given to make low-Calorie meals interesting and tasty. Fats slow the emptying time of the stomach and increase meal satiety, so a low-fat diet will seem more satisfying if fats are distributed throughout the day. Calories will be less concentrated in a low-fat diet, so the diet will be bulkier. Simply from a slimming stand-point, there is no advantage to substituting one type of fat for another.

Vitamins and minerals

The object of a slimming diet is to make certain that the vitamin and mineral requirements of the body are met while the energy requirements of the body are not met. For many slimmers this will mean choosing more nutrient-concentrated sources than previously consumed. A good mixed diet with varied foods from each food group (page 25) will meet the requirements of the body. A good slimming diet will be able to supply adequate vitamins and minerals so that dietary supplements (vitamin pills, tablets) should not be necessary. A slimmer who is making a drastic change of diet may want to take dietary supplements during a short transition period while the body adjusts to the new diet.

Alcohol

Although beer contains some B vitamins and wine contains some iron, alcoholic beverages must be placed in the empty Calorie category of luxury foods on a slimming diet. However, if alcohol is a part of your life, it can be included, in moderation, in a slimming diet.

How fast can you lose?

Weight loss will be erratic and will often seem to show little relationship to food consumption, even for the most dedicated slimmer. For most slimmers, the first kilograms come off easily and should be regarded as encouragement to keep up the good work. However, much of this early weight loss is actually water. Losing fat tissue is a some-what slower process.

The most sensible goal to aim for is an average loss of 1 kg (2.2 lb) a week. The calculations below show why (fig. 4).

These calculations are based on the fact that you must create a deficiency of approximately 3500 Calories to lose 450 g (1 lb). If a woman uses up 2000 Calories a day and keeps to a restricted intake of 1000 Calories, she will only have a deficiency of 1000 Calories a day. At this rate, it will take 3½ days to accumulate the 3500 Calories deficiency required to lose 450 g (1 lb). Just as some people put on weight more easily than others, so people will lose weight at different rates.

If you have a lot of weight to lose, it may be a good idea not to try to lose it too quickly. Over a long period of time it is easy to get fed up with a restrictive diet.

Losing weight gradually improves the chances of ulti-mately keeping off the weight. People who lose weight quickly have not had a chance to develop new eating patterns so gain weight when they return to their old habits.

---

fig. 4

Day 1   2000 Calories used
         − 1000 Calories eaten
         = 1000 Calories   Total deficiency = 1000 Calories
           deficiency

Day 2   2000 Calories used
         − 1000 Calories eaten
         = 1000 Calories   Total deficiency = 2000 Calories
           deficiency

Day 3   2000 Calories used
         − 1000 Calories eaten
         = 1000 Calories   Total deficiency = 3000 Calories
           deficiency

Day 4   2000 Calories used*
         − 1000 Calories eaten
         = 1000 Calories   Total deficiency = 4000 Calories
           deficiency

* 3½ days required for 3500 Calorie deficiency to lose 450 g (1 lb)

33

Gaining weight on a diet

It is possible, though improbable, that you could gain weight adhering to a Calorie restricted diet. Someone totally unaware of their own eating and exercise patterns could just conceivably choose a diet that contained more Calories than their normal diet. (Not to be confused with the fact that many diets will contain more bulk than normal.)

On a day to day basis, weight can be a misleading measure of fat loss. You can lose fat but weigh more if your body is temporarily holding extra water. Until you start weighing yourself regularly during dieting, you may be unaware of day to day fluctuations in weight. It is common to deviate 2.25 kg (5 lb) either up or down because of water gain and loss. Your weight can change by a few kilograms during one day depending upon whether or not you have recently eaten or moved your bowels. Most women weigh a few kilograms heavier just before menstruation as monthly cycles greatly affect water retention in women both before and after menopause.

Water retention is higher on a high carbohydrate diet than on a high protein or high fat diet. If you reduce Calorie intake but increase carbohydrate intake, weight could reflect a slight fluid increase.

Reaching a plateau

Long-term dieters usually reach a stage where weight loss slows down. This is a sign of success. The new smaller body requires less energy than the bigger body did. To continue weight loss, you must increase exercise or further reduce food intake.

Meal patterns for slimming

For successful slimming, choosing *when* to eat may be just as important as choosing *what* to eat.

Importance of breakfast

Giving up breakfast is not a sensible way to cut Calories. Most nutrients are carried to and from cells in the blood in the form of glucose. Blood glucose levels are normally controlled automatically. After a meal, glucose rushes into the bloodstream and the hormone insulin acts to lower the blood glucose level back to normal. If blood glucose levels fall below normal (hypoglycaemia) you may experience weakness, depressed mood, lack of co-ordination and hunger (fig. 5).

Increased accident rate and mental and physical inefficiency are common in breakfast-skippers. Breakfast can help promote a slimmer's sense of well being, lack of hunger and tendency to stick to a diet. However, if your body has adjusted to years without breakfast, slimming may not be the time to change patterns.

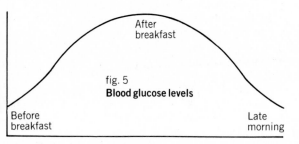

After breakfast

fig. 5
Blood glucose levels

Before breakfast

Late morning

Snacking — the ideal way to slim?

In order to use up a meal the body uses extra energy each time a meal is consumed. The more meals consumed, the more energy used. If you were to eat exactly 1000 Calories you would lose slightly more weight if the 1000 Calories were eaten as six small meals than if it were consumed as three larger meals. In practice, it is easy to cheat and take slightly more Calories by the small meal method. The amount of energy used by this process is small so would be insignificant compared to any increase in food intake.

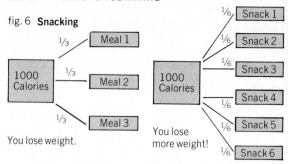

fig. 6 **Snacking**

You lose weight.

You lose more weight!

Snacking can help even out blood glucose levels. Without the extreme ups and downs which result when a huge meal is followed by hours of fasting, a slimmer may feel more satisfied with the frugality of a low-Calorie diet.

Snacking can be a healthy way to slim but only if you choose nutritious snacks. A healthy snack is a salad, a bowl of soup or a sandwich, not a chocolate bar, biscuits or cake. Snacking for slimming only works as a total pattern of eating, not in addition to regular meals (fig. 6).

Plan around your lifestyle
You will only stick to a diet if it fits into your life. No one wants to plan their life around their diet and this is not necessary for slimming. Once you know *when* you eat you can start fitting a slimming diet into your routine. If you eat all the time, a snacking diet (fig. 6) can help you plan to eat often but sensibly. If you eat differently from one day to another (because of different social situations) it may be more manageable to plan dieting on a weekly basis, sticking to 7000-10,500 Calories a week.

Dieters who trust themselves can forget about dieting on special occasions knowing that an overall deficiency of Calories will result in gradual weight loss. A dieter who conscientiously diets all week may not try to diet on weekends. Other slimmers feel it is easier to control appetite if they never allow themselves to over-eat.

Exercise increases BMR and this phenomenon is exaggerated after a meal. To maximize on energy expenditure, meal and exercise patterns should be planned so that meals are followed by periods of activity rather than periods of rest.

Specific slimming diets

Choosing a slimming diet is as personal a matter as choosing a non-slimming diet. The ideal slimming diet will only be a slight modification of an individual's regular diet and will take into consideration personal likes and dislikes and meal patterns. In choosing a slimming diet try to develop a life-long eating pattern which will initially take off weight and then keep off weight.

Slimming diets represent numerous variations of a few basic types of diet. A slimming diet must be based on the principle that you can only lose weight by taking in fewer Calories than you are using. Whatever a diet is called, its aim is to reduce Calorie intake directly or indirectly.

Low-Calorie diets

Calorie intake is monitored directly on a Calorie counting diet. A Calorie limit is set and the individual chooses food and drink adding up to that number of calories. This type of diet is the most flexible as it can be adapted to even the most extraordinary tastes and habits.

To work this type of diet successfully you must accurately record the quantity of all food and drink consumed and look these up in Calorie tables (pages 89-93). At first this process can appear tedious, but most dieters quickly learn to judge portion sizes accurately and learn the Calorie content of foods they eat regularly. Once a pattern of dieting is established, rough calculations will be sufficient to monitor Calorie intake.

You will lose weight whenever the diet supplies fewer Calories than the body is using. On average, a deficit of 500 Calories a day will enable you to lose 450 g (1 lb) a week; a deficit of 1000 Calories a day will enable you to lose 1 kg (2.2 lb) a week. A realistic target for most women is 1000-1500 Calories a day. Because of their higher energy requirements, men can choose higher limits or lose more quickly than women on the lower targets.

The 1500 Calorie limit is appropriate for anyone who normally consumes more than 2000 Calories a day and is physically active. A person with more than 12.5 kg (28 lb) to lose may find it practical to start with a 1500 Calorie diet (page 66) and change to a lower limit when they have reached a plateau. A 1500 Calorie diet may be more realistic for someone with social commitments which involve drinking or entertaining in restaurants.

Everyone should lose weight on a 1000 Calorie diet. Anyone not losing weight on 1000 Calories a day is probably taking in extra Calories by misjudging quantities or forgetting to record everything consumed. The 1000 Calorie limit is appropriate for anyone maintaining weight or gaining weight on fewer than 2000 Calories a day or anyone not physically active. Because of lower energy requirements, many older women need to choose 1000-1200 Calories a day limits to lose weight. The lower Calorie limit is suitable for someone who wants to lose a few kilograms quickly.

Low-carbohydrate diets

Carbohydrates usually make up about half the Calories in the diet. The low-carbohydrate diet indirectly restricts Calories by limiting the carbohydrate intake to about 50 g a day. Some carbohydrate tables give actual carbohydrate values of food. To simplify counting, other tables give carbohydrate units (1 unit equals 5 g carbohydrate) with a 10 carbohydrate unit limit.

By restricting carbohydrates, you cut down on those rich empty-Calorie foods. There is no restriction on carbohydrate-free foods so you can easily choose foods which contain essential nutrients.

Although fats are not monitored, the low carbohydrate diet tends to indirectly limit Calorie concentrated fats by removing the fat carriers from the diet. Most people, for example, use less butter when they cannot spread it on bread, potatoes or pasta.

The low-carbohydrate diet involves fewer calculations than Calorie counting, so it is more suitable for anyone who dislikes arithmetic. This diet is recommended for people with a lot of weight to lose and for people who have not previously tried slimming.

Weight loss will occur only if the diet limits total Calories. The carbohydrate-free foods which are not counted must not contribute too many Calories to the diet. Cheese lovers and nibblers will probably find another diet more suitable.

The low carbohydrate diet has been made popular by

Professor John Yudkin (*This Slimming Business,* Penguin Books 1970) and is a healthy way to slim. This low carbo-hydrate (50 g a day) diet should not be confused with carbohydrate-free diets (Stillman's diet, Atkin's diet) which are *not* recommended.

No-count diets

No-count diets restrict Calories by eliminating high-Calorie foods from the diet. Food is simply divided into three categories. Nutritious foods relatively low in Calories are encouraged (fresh fruit and vegetables, unsweetened beverages, meat, fish, eggs). Nutritious foods relatively high in Calories are recommended in moderation (cheese, milk, starchy vegetables and fruits, fats and oils). High carbohydrate foods (soft drinks, pasta, cakes and potatoes) and alcohol are banned.

The diet is popular with slimmers who do not like calcula-tions and is appropriate for anyone who prefers an 'all or nothing' approach to dieting. This diet only encourages a new pattern of eating if the dieter can make a permanent commitment to avoiding the banned foods.

Fat unit diet

Fats are extremely concentrated sources of energy (256 Calories to 28 g [1 oz]). All diets must reduce fat intake in order to reduce Calorie intake. The fat unit diet directly limits fat consumption. Over 40 per cent of Calories in the diet come from the average 120 g of fat eaten per day. The low-fat diet reduces energy intake by limiting fat to approx-imately 30 g per day.

Fat unit diets set a limit of 10 units a day (1 fat unit equals approximately 3 g fat). Fat unit guides give the fat unit content of all foods regularly consumed. For the most part, all fat-free foods can be eaten in unlimited quantities. To be realistic, the fat unit method gives guidance on how to account for alcohol and sweet foods so that these high-Calorie, fat-free foods do not offset the energy reduc-tion from fat foods.

The diet is sensible as it minimizes the intake of foods which are actually most fattening. The diet encourages the consumption of fruits, vegetables and non-sugary cereal-based foods, and discourages high fat, sugary foods.

One food diet

Magazines are full of diets based on one particular food. These diets have developed for two reasons:

(1) magical properties are attributed to a food's ability to make you lose weight;
(2) a food manufacturer hires a dietitian to design a slimming diet to promote their product.

There are no magical slimming foods but a specific food diet will work if it is designed to lower total Calorie intake. Most fad diets (grapefruit, banana diets, etc.) are not nutritionally balanced and do not develop an appropriate pattern of eating for permanent weight control. However, good long-term diets can be based on one food. One chocolate bar manufacturer promotes a flexible Calorie controlled diet that is built around saving 300 Calories a day for their product. The diet has been popular with slimmers who have a sweet tooth and has sold a lot of chocolate bars.

Regimented diets

Some diets state exactly which foods can be eaten, the quantities of foods to consume, and even the time of day when certain foods are allowed. There is no doubt that these diets work by reducing total Calorie intake but there is nothing magical about the unique prescribed routine. Some people enjoy the discipline involved in following this type of diet. There can be an element of excitement in experimenting with imposed food patterns, but it will not be practical for long-term dieting unless the diet fits into the dieter's lifestyle.

Fasting

Fasting is not recommended as a method of losing weight although fasting for several days is not actually harmful (unless it causes an accident or upsets a health problem). The object of slimming is to reduce the proportion of fat to lean tissue in the body. Long-term fasting uses up lean tissues so can actually increase the ratio of fat to lean tissue.

Fasting obviously does nothing to develop a new eating pattern to keep off weight.

Diet during pregnancy and lactation

A nutrient concentrated diet is particularly important during pregnancy and lactation. Although the requirement for some nutrients (calcium, vitamins C and D) is doubled (Table 8), the energy requirement is only slightly higher in this period.

Nutrient	Non-pregnant	Pregnant 2nd & 3rd trimesters	Lactating
Energy (Calories)	2200	2400	2700
Protein (g)	55	60	68
Calcium (mg)	500	1200	1200
Iron (mg)	12	15	15
Vitamin A (mg)	750	750	1200
Thiamin (mg)	0.9	1.0	1.1
Riboflavin (mg)	1.3	1.6	1.8
Nicotinic acid (mg)	15	18	21
Vitamin C (mg)	30	60	60
Vitamin D (mg)	2.5	10	10

Table 8 Recommended Daily Intake of Nutrients

Department of Health and Social Security

The energy requirements above represent the average requirement for women. Actual requirements vary greatly from one individual to another. Weight gain during pregnancy should be carefully monitored. Doctors disagree on what should be the ideal weight gain, but a woman should probably not gain more than 3.5 kg (8 lb) during the first 20 weeks and gain about 0.4 kg (1 lb) a week thereafter.

Excess weight gain during pregnancy can be harmful to both the woman and her foetus. Because of the special requirements of pregnancy, it is not advisable for a woman to try to slim during pregnancy without medical advice.

A breastfeeding mother will use up approximately 600 Calories a day in producing 800 ml (28 fl oz) of milk. Although some of this extra energy requirement can be taken care of by body fat laid down during pregnancy, at least some of it should be supplied by the diet and milk is a convenient source. A woman who does not consume milk should make certain that her diet contains other good sources of calcium.

SPECIFIC SLIMMING DIETS

Vegetarian slimming diets
The average vegetarian tends to weigh less than the average meat eater, so slimming is certainly possible on a vegetarian diet. Many fruits and vegetables are excellent examples of vitamin and mineral rich, low-Calorie foods. Vegetarian diets tend to contain more fibre (roughage) than meat diets. This roughage adds bulk to the diet and can create a feeling of fullness. The fibre can also prevent constipation common on slimming diets. The legumes (beans, peas, lentils) are rich sources of protein in relation to their Calorie content and vegetables tend to be less expensive sources of protein than meat.

A vegetarian can easily follow a low-Calorie or no-count diet. However, a low-carbohydrate diet will not be appropriate for a vegetarian because of the carbohydrate content of grains, nuts and many vegetables and fruits.

A nutritionally balanced Vegan diet (a vegetarian diet with no milk, cheese, or eggs) is possible with careful thought and vitamin B_{12} supplements. A diet containing no animal products will be cholesterol-free and will be low in saturated fats.

Diabetes and slimming
Obesity, particularly gross obesity, often causes the development of diabetes in people with a genetic tendency to the disease. Weight loss can reduce complications of diabetes and in some cases dietary control can reduce the need for insulin injections. Diabetic dietary treatment often involves a low-carbohydrate diet distributed as small meals throughout the day (a low-carbohydrate 'snacking' diet). This diet can, of course, easily be adapted as a low-Calorie diet appropriate to slimmers whether or not they are diabetic.

Diet and aging
Obesity is particularly common in the elderly, because of their reduced energy requirements. Nutrient requirements may be greater in the elderly and the absorption of nutrients from foods is not as efficient as in younger people. Therefore the ideal diet for an older person will be a nutrient rich low-Calorie diet. Obesity can aggravate problems of arthritis, rheumatism, and respiratory infections in the elderly.

Children and slimming

Keeping off weight is easier than losing weight at any stage of life, so childhood weight control is a good investment for later years. Although some overweight children outgrow their chubbiness, many will have to consciously change their eating habits or grow into fat adolescents and fat adults.

Childhood obesity reflects the changing pattern of obesity in our society. Five to fifteen per cent of children are overweight and the prevalence of obesity is growing. Social class differences in obesity emerge early. An American study showed that at the age of 6-7, 8 per cent of girls from lower socio-economic groups were obese, but none of the upper-class girls were overweight.

Weight control begins in the first days of a child's life. Bottle-fed babies are more likely to be overfed than breast-fed babies and the early introduction of solid foods can lead to overfeeding. Fat babies get a bad start to life as the developing body may have difficulty coping with too much fat. Fat babies are slower to walk and stand. Flat feet, knock knees, back problems, and breathing difficulties are common in overweight children. Even in a society aware of the dangers of obesity, fat cuddly babies are admired.

At an early age, babies and children should be encouraged to explore and enjoy physical activity; exercise can play an important role in a child's weight control. Usually, non-obese children are much more active than obese children.

Helping a child to slim can be a challenge. A special diet must not set a child apart from friends and family. A diet must be designed to meet the nutritional needs of a growing body, but at the same time encourage new eating patterns appropriate to the child's energy requirements. (Cooking to Make Kids Slim by Audrey Ellis, Stanley Paul, London 1976 is recommended as a good source of ideas.)

Treating the psychological causes and consequences of a child's obesity may be more urgent than treating physical aspects of the problem. A child's self-image and relationship to others will be greatly influenced by being overweight. Children can be immensely cruel to an overweight playmate. Rejecting or devouring food can be an important sense of power for a child.

Slimming aids

No special gadgets, powders, solutions or foods are required for slimming, but some slimmers find them useful.
The slimmers' market represents a huge potential for new
products because at any one time millions of people are
slimming or trying to slim. The same companies which
produce regular foods to fatten us up, then offer us special
products for slimming.

Inevitably the use of special products adds to the cost of
slimming. Some products take advantage of a slimmer's
lack of knowledge. Calorie-counted products tend to be
more expensive even when they do not contain fewer
Calories than similar foods. If nutritional information
(Calories, carbohydrate, fat, protein content) were required on all foods, slimmers could more easily use regular
products in their slimming diets.

A product which controls portion size and minimizes
food preparation will be useful for those tempted by tasting
and nibbling when preparing foods or who cannot resist
left-overs. Nature offers a wide range of portion controlled
convenience foods: eggs, oranges, tomatoes, fish, etc.

Meal substitutes

A number of Calorie-controlled products are now available
to replace one or more meals a day. These products work
simply by helping to reduce total Calorie intake and have no
special slimming properties if they are taken in addition to
regular meals. Only if you learn to design your own low-
Calorie meals, will these products be helpful in estab-
lishing a permanent pattern of eating.

Complete slimmers' meals are available as dehydrated
meals in a packet, frozen or tinned products (Contour,
Nutriplan, Kousa, Findus, Dietade). These products are
useful for someone who has no idea about Calorie counting.
However, they do not represent particularly low-Calorie or
inexpensive meals. These meals may be enriched with
extra vitamins or minerals, but these should not be needed
if you choose a sensible diet.

Special *slimming biscuits* (Limmits, Trimetts, Bisks)
are available in both sweet and savoury form and are
designed to replace a meal. These biscuits sometimes

contain more Calories than conventional biscuits. But often they also contain methyl cellulose, and extra vitamins and minerals. Methyl cellulose, a bulking agent, is supposed to make the stomach feel full but it is questionable whether it works. As for the added nutrients, there is something drastically wrong with a slimming diet dependent on biscuits for vitamins and minerals!

Slimming drinks (formula diets), to replace one or more meals, are designed to provide essential nutrients in low-Calorie portions. Healthy people can use slimming drinks to totally replace meals for short periods to achieve a quick weight loss. But the diet is monotonous and the lack of roughage could cause constipation. It is not advisable to regularly consume less than 1000 Calories a day without medical supervision and anyone with heart disease, kidney disease, or diabetes should not live on formula diets without medical advice.

Imitation foods

Low-Calorie versions of regular foods are the most useful aid for many slimmers. Sugar (sucrose) contains 110 Calories per 28 g (1 oz) but no valuable nutrients, so the object of any slimming diet is to minimize sugar intake. Both cyclamate and saccharin have been popular *sugar replacements* as they contain no Calories but are very sweet. Compared to sucrose, cyclamate is 30 times sweeter; saccharin is 300-550 times sweeter. Cyclamates have been withdrawn from the market in many countries because of controversy over the health risk of large quantities. Saccharin is available as virtually Calorie-free liquids and pellets (Hermesetas, Sweetex, Saxin) or mixed with sugar or sorbitol as low-Calorie powders and granules (Sweetex, Sweet 'n Low, Slimcea, Sucron, Sugar-Lite). Low-Calorie drinks, where saccharin replaces sugar, are popular with slimmers.

Sugar substitutes do help to cut down Calories, but they do nothing to minimize the craving for sweet foods and drinks. In the long term it is best to work at reducing sugar intake and limit sweet-tasting foods and drinks in the diet so that you become less tempted by sweets.

Slimmers should not confuse saccharin with sorbitol. Sorbitol tastes less sweet than sugar (sucrose) and is useful in diabetic diets, but sorbitol contains nearly as many Calories as sugar so is of no special value for slimming.

Slimming breads (Nimble, Procea, Slimcea) contain more air than ordinary breads, so have approximately two thirds the Calories per slice. If exactly the same number of slices are eaten, slimming bread will reduce Calorie intake. However, there is no advantage to slimming breads if more slices than usual are consumed. Extra slices that carry extra butter or jam will increase Calorie intake. Because of the bulk of wholemeal bread, many slimmers find they feel satisfied eating less wholemeal bread than white bread and the roughage is useful for preventing constipation.

Fat is a very concentrated source of Calories so *low-fat versions of food* are useful in cutting Calories. Low-fat spreads (Outline) dilute margarine or butter with water and cut the Calories in half. (You can make your own (page 60) as this is an expensive way to buy water!) The fat portion of milk can be removed without affecting the valuable calcium and protein content. Such skimmed milks and skimmed milk powders (Marvel) have only half the Calories of full-fat milk. These products must not be confused with milk powders (Five Pints) where vegetable fat has been substituted for animal fat. Low-fat versions of salad dressings (Waistline, Heinz) and ice-cream type desserts (Slim-Ice, Lyons) are also available.

Appetite depressants

Appetite depressants are taken before a meal to reduce hunger. Some contain glucose (Ayds) and work by raising the blood glucose level so that the slimmer does not feel hungry. Many ordinary foods or sweets would work in the same way. Other products contain methyl cellulose (Trihextin, Pastils 808, Slim Discs) which is supposed to expand in the stomach and give a feeling of fullness. Slimmers seldom find that methyl cellulose reduces appetite.

Laxatives

Laxatives do not help slimming and are not recommended. The object of slimming is to reduce fat, not to rush food through the system so that you weigh less the moment you are weighed.

Slimming groups

Many slimmers experience dieting as an isolated individual 'problem' and find it useful to have other people take an interest in their slimming. Slimming groups have been formed so that slimmers can exchange information and offer support to each other. There is a wide range of groups. Progressive doctors and health workers may help overweight patients to form a slimming group. Groups can grow out of adult education slimming classes or Women's Therapy Centres can set up Compulsive Eating groups.

A number of commercial slimming groups are now popular (Weight Watchers, Silhouette, Slimming Magazine). These groups usually charge a membership fee and a fee for the regular classes or meetings. Group meetings include a talk and discussion, and possibly exercise. A group leader helps each individual to choose a target weight, slimming diet and gives regular encouragement. Some groups choose a diet to fit an individual's lifestyle. Other groups give the same regimented diet to all members.

Slimming with a doctor's help

A doctor may be able to help someone who finds it impossible to lose weight by dieting and exercise but is worried by the health risks of obesity. Drugs are available which work to accelerate the metabolic rate or to reduce appetite, but these must be used under very strict medical supervision. In severe cases, a doctor can clamp the jaws closed so that the patient can only consume a Calorie-controlled liquid diet. Although such drastic measures can help someone lose weight, a person will still have to develop a new eating pattern to keep off unwanted weight. In an emergency, a major surgical operation can be performed to remove part of the intestine so that less food can be absorbed into the body.

Slimming and exercise

One way of increasing the energy gap, that is, using up more energy than there is in the food you eat, is to exercise. Combined with a slimming diet, exercise will not only help you lose weight more quickly than no exercise at all, but will make you feel fitter and trimmer, and by improving muscle tone will give you a better, firmer figure. As the kilograms roll off you will find that, with regular exercise, you can avoid the problem of slack skin and muscle, which will make you feel flabby even though you may have lost all the weight you wanted to lose.

In western countries lack of exercise is a widespread problem because our urban way of life means that we rely to a great extent on automation and mechanization: we ride to work in cars, buses or trains, use lifts and escalators instead of the stairs, work sitting at a desk all day, and spend most of our leisure time watching television. Because we rarely need to make a sustained physical effort in order to do things, many of us have lost the habit and the will for anything but sedentary activity. But there are many positive reasons for taking up some form of exercise, apart from the fact that it will help you to slim.

As well as the benefits mentioned above, exercise improves the circulation and respiration, increasing the supply of blood and oxygen to the muscles, including the heart muscle. This improvement means that, after only a relatively short period of taking regular exercise, you will find that less effort is required for other activities, and that you have more stamina and energy than ever before. Physical effort of all kinds will become easier, you will get tired less quickly, and you will be able to stay active into old age. Exercise also helps to counteract stress and tension, and will help you sleep better. It has been found that people who exercise regularly are less likely to have a heart attack, and much research is being done into the other benefits of exercise on the bodily processes.

Once you have begun, you will find that exercise can be enormously enjoyable. This enjoyment factor will improve your sense of well-being which, along with the physical benefits, will improve the posture, which will make you look slimmer.

How to begin

If you are not in the habit of exercising, you may find that the greatest obstacle to actually beginning is setting aside the time each day to do it. If at any time you feel your willpower flagging and need spurring on, re-read the preceding section. For exercise to be effective as part of your slimming programme it must be regular and fairly vigorous.

If you are not used to exercise, start off gently and slowly, gradually increasing the time and effort spent on the activity, so that eventually you are spending at least half an hour daily in quite strenuous movement. The first effect will be aching muscles, but you will soon start to feel better after each session than you did before it. Any convenient time of day is suitable, except the hour after a meal.

Ways to exercise

One way to take extra exercise is simply to increase the amount of energy exerted naturally in the normal course of a day. For example, walk rather than drive or catch a bus, use the stairs rather than the lift. Gardening, housework and do-it-yourself activities all offer scope for vigorous exercise. Slow walking uses up about 270 Calories an hour, whereas brisk walking uses up about 440 Calories an hour, the same as an hour's swimming or climbing.

Another way of exercising is to do specific activities for which you set aside time, and these can be either in the form of a sport or a non-competitive activity such as running or jogging, swimming, tennis, cycling, skipping or stair-climbing. The aim of all these forms of exercise is to raise the pulse rate enough to make you out of breath at the end of 15 minutes or so (sooner when you are beginning) and this should be a guide to the amount of effort you put into the activity. Do not attempt too much too quickly, and always stop if you feel at all uncomfortable; your body will tell you how far to go. Take particular care if you are very overweight or over 35 and have previously been inactive. It is a good idea to set yourself targets, increasing distance and speed gradually. Aim to exercise at least three times a week, increasing distance before increasing speed, and only moving a stage further after you have reached your present stage several times in reasonable comfort. Always wear clothes that allow freedom of movement.

Keep-fit exercises

The 12 keep-fit exercises shown here are not a formal course but merely a selection for different parts of the body. They may be done in any order except for the first five which are for limbering up. Choose the ones best for you, building up to the full number of repeats gradually. They are all designed for both men and women, even though the female form is illustrated here.

1: Head-circling

Stand erect with feet apart, hands on hips.

Continue moving head round in a circle.

Pull chin in and move head round to shoulder.

Repeat movement 10 times in each direction.

2: Arm circling

Stand erect with the feet comfortably apart. Circle both arms simultaneously, swinging them backwards over your head 10 times, then forwards 10 times.

3: Trunk-twisting

Stand erect, feet apart, arms loosely by the sides. Moving from the hips, twist the trunk and head to the left and then, with a swinging movement, to the right. Repeat the movement 10 times.

4: Toe-touching

Stand erect, feet apart. Bend down to touch toes, legs straight if possible.

Return to upright position between each toe-touching. Repeat 10 times.

5: Knee bends

Stand erect, feet apart. Bend one knee and bring it up towards your chest, pulling it in as far as you

can with both hands. Do the same with the other knee, and repeat 10 times with each knee.

6: Leg raising

Lie flat on your back with your arms straight by your sides. Keeping the legs straight, raise each one alternately until it is vertical. Repeat up to 20 times with each leg.

From the same position, raise both legs at once, keeping them straight. Repeat 15 times.

7: Sit-ups

Lie on your back and rise up from the hips to a near-sitting position without using arms, till hands touch knees. Lie back and repeat 20 times.

8: Overhead stretches

Stand erect with feet apart at shoulder width.

Bend to the right, right arm above you, palm up.

Repeat to the left, with left arm overhead.

Return to upright position and repeat 10 times.

9: Waist circles

Stand with feet apart, arms overhead and thumbs crossed.

Start to swing the arms down, bending the knees.

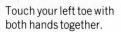

Twist round from the waist so that you face left.

Touch your left toe with both hands together.

Swing to the right and touch your right toe.

Swing round and up. Do five in each direction.

10: Sitting toe-touching

Sit upright on the floor, legs straight and apart and arms outstretched.

Stretch the right hand towards the left toe, touching it if possible.

Stretch left hand towards right toe, again touching it if possible. Repeat 10 times in a smooth movement.

11: Hip walking

Sit on floor, hands on knees, and move forward on hips, bending legs.

Repeat, going backwards, taking 10 'steps' in each direction.

12: Astride-jumps

Stand erect with the feet together and hands on hips. Jump the feet apart sideways and bring them together again as you land (left).

Repeat the whole movement smoothly and rhythmically, without pausing, 20 or 30 times. A variation is to raise the arms sideways as you jump.

Slimming — in the kitchen

The way food is cooked makes a considerable difference to the number of Calories consumed. It is not necessary to eat lettuce and carrots three times a day — just choose the right foods and put into practice the following guidelines.

A recipe for Coq au Vin shows how a traditional chicken dish can use up half a day's diet Calorie allowance (even without accompaniments). With certain amendments to ingredients and method the Calories can be halved.

Ingredients to Serve 4	Calories for 1 Portion
1 × 1.5kg/3lb chicken	250
bouquet garni	—
salt and black pepper	—
100 g/4oz/½ cup chopped streaky bacon	115
100g/4oz/¼lb button mushrooms	5
2 cloves garlic crushed	—
100g/4oz/¼lb button onions	5
50g/2oz/¼ cup unsalted butter	105
1 tablespoon oil	30
2 tablespoons brandy	20
600ml/1 pint/2½ cups red wine	100
300ml/½ pint/1¼ cups stock	5
beurre manié	50
Total without garnish	685

Coq au Vin (Low-Calorie Version)

Ingredients to Serve 4	Calories for 1 Portion
1 × 1.5kg/3lb chicken	200
salt and black pepper	—
300 ml/½ pint/1¼ cups red wine	50
2 cloves garlic, crushed	—
2 teaspoons oil	15
100g/4oz/¼lb button onions	5
100g/4oz/¼lb button mushrooms	5
300ml/½ pint/1¼ cups stock	5
1 tablespoon cornflour (cornstarch)	15
1 tablespoon water	—
chopped parsley, to garnish	
Total Calories per portion including garnish	295

Cut the chicken into 4 joints and remove the skin. Mix together the next 7 ingredients to make a marinade. Soak the chicken in this for several hours. Strain, reserve the marinade. Place the chicken in a casserole dish and cook uncovered in a moderately hot oven (190°C/375°F, Gas Mark 5) for 30 minutes. Remove from the oven, pour over the marinade and stock, then cover the casserole. Lower the temperature to moderate (180°C/350°F, Gas Mark 4) and cook the casserole for 45 minutes to 1 hour. Remove the chicken joints and vegetables and keep warm on a serving dish. Strain the liquid into a saucepan and reduce to 300ml/½ pint/1¼ cups. Blend the cornflour (cornstarch) with cold water. Add the reduced liquor, stir and return to the pan. Heat, stirring until the sauce thickens.

Fats – keep out!

Fats are a group of foods which should be carefully watched by those wishing to slim. Some fat in the diet is essential but even if all visible fat is removed there is no danger of our going short, as there is much hidden fat in many foods. Meat has a high proportion of hidden fat so remove any that is visible before cooking. Brown the meat in its own fat and drain off any excess. The use of roasting bags and foil enables meat to cook in its own juices which provides extra flavour without adding fat. If possible, cook casseroles in advance, cool, then skim fat which has risen to the top.

Grill, poach or steam food rather than fry. For essential frying such as browning and omelets, use a good non-stick pan. Chips absorb a considerable amount of fat; though oven chips are lower in Calories, and grilling them reduces the Calories further. Roast potatoes are best avoided but remember that smaller pieces of potato absorb more fat!

Sauces and gravy usually have a high proportion of fat which can be reduced by thickening liquids with cornflour (cornstarch) and using gravy powder or granules with vegetable water. For soups and stews extra vegetables can be used for thickening.

Butter and margarine should be kept soft for spreading as less will be used. Low-Calorie spreads make a useful alternative as they contain half the Calories per tablespoon. These can also be used for gentle cooking. It is possible to make your own low-Calorie fat for spreading (not suitable for frying) by creaming together 25g/1oz/2 tablespoons margarine with 2 tablespoons boiling water.

Although cheese is classed as a protein food most varieties are about one third fat. Dutch cheeses, notably Edam, contain less, giving about 90 Calories to 25g/1oz/¼ cup compared with 120 to 130 for other hard cheeses. Cottage cheese is made from skim milk so contains virtually no fat: curd cheese contains 10 to 30 per cent fat but cream cheeses have over 80 per cent, so avoid! In most recipes cottage or curd cheese can successfully be substituted for cream cheese. Where possible cream should be avoided in cooking and on desserts. The worst Calorie offenders are clotted, double (heavy) and whipping cream. Single (light) and sour cream are better but should only be taken in moderation. Suitable alternatives are natural (unflavored) yogurt or evaporated milk.

Sugars – beware!
Sugar provides nothing but empty Calories in the diet so it should be omitted whenever possible. Sugar substitutes provide a good alternative in drinks and desserts.

Granulated and powder sugar substitutes are marketed under various brand names. Basically they consist of small granules of sugar coated with saccharin to increase their sweetness, which varies with each brand. Weight for weight the substitutes do not contain less Calories but a saving is made by using smaller quantities.

Fructose occurs naturally in some fruits and vegetables and in honey. Although its Calorie count is similar to sugar it is the sweetest of all the sugars. It can mask the bitterness of saccharin, so a combination of fructose and saccharin makes the ideal sugar substitute.

Canned fruits contain a high proportion of sugar in the syrup, so this should be drained. Some manufacturers are now canning fruit in natural juice which gives less Calories and a better taste. Squashes and fizzy drinks contain a high proportion of sugar (1 teaspoon to a glass of fruit squash) so change to the low-Calorie varieties which have a negligible number of Calories (no more than 12 Cals per 300ml/½ pint/1¼ cups when made up). The squashes can also be used in cooking. Beware of fresh fruit juices which can provide up to 50 Calories a glass.

Cereals and wholefoods – in moderation!

It is essential to have some cereals in the diet to provide bulk and roughage, but they are not low in Calories so should be taken in moderation. Breakfast cereals provide a quick simple meal but avoid the sugar varieties and choose those containing bran which provide extra fibre.

Bread contains many useful nutrients. Wholemeal bread has marginally less Calories than white, but it has the advantages of providing more roughage and of being more satisfying. Low-Calorie breads can be useful as long as they are substituted slice for slice with ordinary bread.

By using wholefoods such as wholemeal flour, wholemeal pasta and brown rice in the diet, meals will become more satisfying without extra Calories. Remember that wholefoods have similar Calorie values to the white alternatives but less should be required to satisfy hunger.

Meat and fish – a few points to watch

Pork, lamb and beef are higher in Calories than offal, chicken and turkey. Most of the fat in poultry is contained in the skin so remove this. Beware of poultry such as duck and goose which have a high fat content. Sausages, beefburgers and other meat products have starch and extra fat added so they are relatively high in Calories.

Fish makes an excellent alternative to meat as it is generally lower in Calories, cooks more quickly and is easier to digest. White fish such as plaice (flounder), cod or haddock have a lower calorific value than the oily fish such as mackerel and herring.

Vegetables and fruit – a little caution!

Vegetables should be cooked very quickly in a little salted boiling water. It is better to have them slightly undercooked as the extra chewing will give you the feeling of having eaten more. Vegetables will absorb large quantities of fat so it is better not to fry them. Vegetable purées make a good base for soups, sauces and stews. Salads lend much variety to a meal but beware of dressings; stick to low-Calorie dressings and those based on yogurt.

The average portion of fresh fruit contains about 40 to 50 Calories so it should not be eaten without restraint. Ones to watch are bananas, grapes, cherries and nectarines.

Further hints for the slimmer

As the kitchen is the area of temptation, avoid being there any more than is necessary. By planning menus well ahead, much of the preparation and cooking can be done in intensive sessions. If you must have cakes, biscuits and other fattening foods in the house, keep them in an inconvenient place. A further precaution is to stick labels on the containers saying 'NO'. Memory jogging photographs of you the 'heavyweight' could also help. Keep the amount of weight you hope to lose displayed as bags of potatoes, flour, or sugar, then reduce the pile as you lose weight.

Even diet meals should be social occasions so sit and eat with the family or a companion whenever possible. Try to fill the plate, eat slowly and chew the food well.

If hunger pangs just will not go away, have a low-Calorie drink, black tea or coffee, suck a fruit gum (2 to 3 Calories each) or clean your teeth with a refreshing toothpaste. Children's teatime may be the most dangerous time so it is worth reserving some of the day's Calories for this.

Shopping

Never shop when you are tired and hungry as you will spend more money and buy more of the wrong foods. It is better to plan menus and make a shopping list, then stick to it. It is also worth planning a route around the supermarket as temptation increases the more 'fattening foods' are seen. If possible, do not take young children as you may feel obliged to bribe them with snack foods.

Foods have already been discussed but many ready-made products contain concealed fat and starch. Go easy on nuts, crisps, dessicated coconut, mayonnaise and dressings. Salami, liver sausage, luncheon meat, sausage rolls and pasties all have a high fat and Calorie value. Sauces and pickles contain a high proportion of sugar. Sugary drinks are not good for anyone in the family so keep to fruit juices and low-Calorie alternatives.

Convenience substitute meals and low-Calorie ready packed meals are an expensive way to diet but they can be useful when morale is low and the temptation to indulge is great! By eating only the contents of the packet you know exactly how many Calories have been used and no further calculations are necessary.

Eating out and parties

Eating in restaurants can cause some problems for those on a diet but there is no need to refuse invitations and be unsociable. With careful planning, not too many Calories need be spent. The chart overleaf gives some indication of the dishes to avoid and those to choose.

Unfortunately, very few restaurants cater for the slimmer, even worse, most of the dishes include more fat, alcohol, pastry (dough) and rich sauces than would be used in the domestic kitchen. Portions are often larger.

As a general guide, choose the plain simple dishes, grilled rather than fried, and avoid all rich sauces or pastry (dough). The most suitable accompaniments to the main course are a plain side salad with little or no dressing, or a green vegetable with no added butter. Refuse chips, sauté potatoes, roast potatoes or pasta and just have a little plain boiled rice or one boiled potato. For dessert stick to simple fruit based dishes or fresh fruit. At all costs ignore cream, cheesecakes, pastries, gâteaux and meringues.

When eating out there is a great temptation to over-eat so try not to eat more than you really feel you need. While waiting for the food to arrive do not nibble bread rolls with butter or bread-sticks which could amount to 200 Calories. Allow yourself one to two glasses of dry wine, but ask for a glass of water to sip or use it to dilute the wine. Even with careful planning you will probably consume more Calories than usual so try to save up by cutting down beforehand.

Parties require a different approach as the food is not the main reason for socializing. The danger areas are the constant drinking of alcohol and nibbling snacks such as peanuts and crisps. Beware of punches which contain varying quantities of wine, spirits, fruit juices, lemonade and sugar. Try to stick to dry white wine, martini or sherry topped with lots of soda or low-Calorie mixers. Even a low-Calorie tonic with lemon looks alcoholic! See the alcohol chart on page 94 for some idea of how many Calories can be consumed in drinks.

If you know that there is to be no meal provided, eat before arriving at the party. This should help to avoid the temptation of nibbles: a small handful of peanuts amounts to 200 Calories with crisps, potato snacks and cheese also rating high on the Calorie charts.

The Calories given in the charts below are for an average restaurant portion, but these can vary enormously.

Foods to avoid		Foods to choose	
Starters		*Starters*	
Pâté with toast & butter	600	Grapefruit half	15
Avocado with prawns	450	Consommé	60
Fried whitebait	300	Tomato Juice	20
Taramasalata with		Orange Juice	60
bread	400	Melon Slice	50
Cream soups	300-400	Moules Marinière	150
Lobster bisque	400	Artichoke with	
Smoked salmon with		vinaigrette	175
bread and butter	350	Humous	175
Main Meals		*Main Meals*	
Risotto	700	Charcoal kebabs	350-400
Paella	700	Calves' liver in sauce	340
Lasagne	650	Barbecue spare ribs	180
Moussaka	690	Ham salad	250
Duck in orange sauce	800	Chicken casserole	500
Beef curry	1000	Quiche Lorraine	350-400
Sole meunière	720	Plain omelet	200
Wiener schnitzel	700	Egg and cheese salad	350
Chicken chop suey	505	Steak tartare (small)	325
Steak pie & chips	1225	225g/½lb grilled steak	400
Egg & chips	550		
Pizza	600		
Ploughman's			
lunch	800-1000		
Desserts		*Desserts*	
Crêpes Suzette with		Fresh fruit	40-50
cream	400	Lemon sorbet	80-100
Christmas pudding		Crème Caramel	150
with cream	600	Lychees in syrup	120
Bakewell tart	500	Plain ice cream	150
Treacle tart with		Baked apple	150
custard	600	Fruit mousse	80-100
Profiteroles with cream	400	25g/1oz French or	
Milles feuilles gâteau	450	Italian cheese	100
Ice cream with nuts			
and chocolate	400		

Diet plan and recipes

The following two week diet plan is based on 1500 Calories a day which should allow for a gradual weight loss. This is preferable to a drastic weight loss where the weight is more likely to be put back on again. If you wish to cut down further, you can reduce your intake to 1200 or 1000 Calories a day after a few weeks. If in any doubt about your health, it is wise to consult a doctor.

The diet is based on three meals allowing about 200 Calories for breakfast, 300 for lunch and 500 for dinner. The milk and butter allowance add another 300, leaving 200 to use as you wish. Consult the Calorie charts for ideas. Any amount of water, tea or coffee can be drunk but other drinks should be added into your calculations.

The starred recipes in the diet can be found on pages 68 - 88. They are for four persons, but the Calorie values given at the beginning of each recipe are for one serving only (rounded up to the nearest 5). If you are cooking for one, it is probably easier to halve the recipe, eat one portion and reserve the other for the next day, or freeze it for future use. Non-dieters can fill up on potatoes or pasta.

You may prefer to make up your own diet plan using the following recipes plus help from the Calorie charts for the basic foods. However, there are basic guidelines essential to a successful diet. Plan three meals a day, allowing some Calories for between meal snacks. At each meal serve animal or vegetable protein. During each day include two portions of fresh vegetables or salad, at least one piece of fresh fruit, one or two slices of bread (preferably wholemeal), 300ml/½ pint/1 cup milk and a thin spread of butter or margarine.

It is advisable to weigh food at first in order to make an accurate Calorie count. After a while your eye will become trained and you will not have to weigh everything. When making up the recipes, weigh all the foods for best results and a more accurate Calorie count. Follow the metric, imperial or American quantities — do not mix them. Fresh herbs are used in the recipes unless otherwise stated. If you substitute dried herbs, halve the quantities stated. Use freshly ground black pepper wherever pepper is specified. Ovens should be preheated to the specified temperature.

Menus for a 14-day, 1500 calorie diet

The following represent a daily allowance of additional foods which should be incorporated in the diet plan.

1. 300ml/½ pint/1¼ cups milk or 600ml/1 pint/2½ cups skimmed milk.

2. 7g/¼oz/½ tablespoon butter or 15g/½oz/1 tablespoon low-fat spread.

3. 200 Calories for snacks or extra portions and drink other than water, tea or coffee.

Breakfast

The following breakfast menus supply about 200 Calories excluding milk and butter from the allowance given above. Choose whichever you like but do not eat more than one egg per day.

1. 25g/1oz/1 cup cornflakes or similar cereal; 1 teaspoon sugar; 120ml/4 fl oz/½ cup fresh orange juice.

2. 25g/1oz/1 cup porridge oats: 2 teaspoons sugar or honey; ½ grapefruit.

3. 1 boiled egg; 1 slice wholemeal toast; 1 teaspoon marmalade; 120ml/4 fl oz/½ cup fresh grapefruit juice.

4. 2 streaky rashers bacon grilled (broiled); 1 tomato grilled (broiled); 1 slice wholemeal toast; 120ml/4 fl oz/½ cup fresh orange juice.

5. 75g/3oz/⅓ cup cottage cheese; 1 slice wholemeal bread; 120ml/4 fl oz/½ cup fresh grapefruit juice.

6. 150ml/¼ pint/⅔ cup natural (unflavored) yogurt with 1 teaspoon honey and 1 tablespoon raisins; 1 slice wholemeal bread.

7. 1 small banana mixed with 150ml/¼ pint/⅔ cup fruit yogurt and 1 tablespoon bran.

Lunch and Dinner

These menus compliment each other to give a balanced diet for the day. Transpose the lunch and dinner if you prefer.

Week 1	*Lunch*	*Dinner*
Monday	40g/1½oz/⅓ cup hard cheese 2 cracker biscuits	Barbecued liver* Tomato salad (dressing*)

	1 piece cucumber	Baked bananas with orange*
	1 apple	
Tuesday	Vegetable hotpot*	Orange and lemon chicken*
	25g/1oz/¼ cup grated cheese	Crunchy coleslaw*
	1 fresh peach	Sultana baked apple*
Wednesday	Cottage cheese and nut platter*	Pork and orange kebabs*
	1 slice wholemeal bread	Green salad (dressing*)
		Apricot fool*
Thursday	50g/2oz/¼ cup lean ham	Tomato smoked haddock*
	1 tomato	2 boiled potatoes
	2 slices wholemeal bread	6 tablespoons French beans
	2 plums	Grape brûlée*
Friday	Toasted pizza*	Chicken parcel*
	Crunchy coleslaw*	1 jacket potato (medium)
	1 pear	tomato salad (dressing*)
		150ml/¼ pint/⅔ cup fruit yogurt
Saturday	Farmhouse omelet*	175g/6oz lean roast beef
	1 slice wholemeal bread	1 small roast potato
	1 apple	3 tablespoons cauliflower
		2 heads broccoli
		2 tablespoons gravy
		Apricot fool*
Sunday	Savoury spinach bake*	Mushroom and yogurt lamb*
	1 slice wholemeal bread	2 tablespoons peas
	1 orange	2 tablespoons carrots
		Cœur à la crème*

67

DIET PLAN

Week 2

Monday	75g/3oz/¹⁄₃ cup tuna (drained of oil) 1 slice wholemeal bread 1 tomato, lettuce 12 grapes	Barbecued liver* 3 tablespoons boiled rice 2 tablespoons carrots Blackcurrant fluff*
Tuesday	Egg and bean savoury* 1 slice wholemeal bread 1 tomato 1 orange	Turkey curry* 6 tablespoons boiled rice Eastern cucumber salad* Tomato salad (dressing*) Plums with meringue topping*
Wednesday	Farmhouse omelet* 1 slice wholemeal bread 1 tomato 1 orange	Orange and lemon chicken* 2 boiled potatoes Red cabbage salad* Blackberry sorbet*
Thursday	50g/2oz/¹⁄₄ cup corned beef 1 slice wholemeal bread 1 tomato, lettuce 150ml/¹⁄₄ pint/²⁄₃ cup natural (unflavored) yogurt	Vegetable rissoles* Cucumber and tomato salad (dressing*) 50g/2oz/¹⁄₄ cup mashed potato 50g/2oz/¹⁄₄ cup ice cream 100g/4oz/1 cup strawberries
Friday	40g/1¹⁄₂oz/¹⁄₃ cup hard cheese 2 cracker biscuits 1 tomato 1 apple	Kidneys in lemon sauce* 4 tablespoons cooked rice Tomato salad (dressing*) Grape brûlée*

68

Saturday	Vegetable hotpot* 25g/1oz/¼ cup grated cheese 1 fresh orange 1 slice wholemeal bread	175g/6oz roast lean pork 1 small roast potato 4 tablespoons cabbage 2 tablespoons thin gravy Blackcurrant fluff*
Sunday	Celery soup* 1 slice wholemeal bread Stuffed peppers* 100g/4oz/1 cup strawberries	Sweet and sour cod steaks* 1 jacket potato (medium) 2 tablespoons peas 4 tablespoons French beans 150ml/¼ pint/⅔ cup fruit yogurt

Starters and snacks

Chilled Tomato and Cucumber Soup   70 Cals

Metric/Imperial	*American*
225/8oz cucumber, peeled	2 cups peeled cucumber
½ green pepper, cored, seeded	½ green pepper, cored seeded
2 cloves garlic, crushed	2 cloves garlic, crushed
salt and pepper	salt and pepper
300ml/½ pint natural yogurt	1¼ cups unflavored yogurt
150ml/¼ pint skimmed milk	⅔ cup skimmed milk
150ml/¼ pint tomato juice	⅔ cup tomato juice
chopped parsley, to garnish	chopped parsley, to garnish

Place all the ingredients except the parsley in an electric blender and work until smooth. Chill. Serve sprinkled with parsley.

Toasted Pizzas
200 Cals

Metric/Imperial
4 slices low-Calorie bread
15g/½oz low-Calorie
  spread
100g/4oz Cheddar cheese,
  grated
4 tomatoes, sliced
1 teaspoon dried oregano
salt and pepper
50g/2oz lean ham, cut into
  strips
4 black olives, sliced

American
4 slices low-Calorie bread
1 tablespoon low-Calorie
  spread
1 cup grated Cheddar
  cheese
4 tomatoes, sliced
1 teaspoon dried oregano
salt and pepper
2 slices lean ham, cut into
  strips
4 ripe olives, sliced

Toast the bread lightly on both sides and cover with the low-Calorie spread. Arrange half the cheese on the toast then top with the tomato slices. Sprinkle with the oregano, salt and pepper to taste. Top with the remaining cheese, then arrange the ham over the top. Place the olive slices in between the ham. Place the pizzas under a preheated moderate grill until the cheese has melted. Serve immediately.

Grapefruit Cocktail
25 Cals

Metric/Imperial
2 large grapefruit, halved
½ carrot, grated
2.5cm/1 inch piece of
  cucumber, diced
½ green pepper, cored,
  seeded and chopped
½ red pepper, cored,
  seeded and chopped
grated rind of ½ orange
black pepper

American
2 large grapefruit, halved
½ carrot, grated
1 inch piece of cucumber,
  diced
½ green pepper, cored,
  seeded and chopped
½ red pepper, cored,
  seeded and chopped
grated rind of ½ orange
black pepper

Remove the flesh from the grapefruit halves, leaving the shells intact. Remove the pith from the fruit, chop and place in a bowl with the juice. Add the remaining ingredients with pepper to taste and mix well. Chill. Just before serving pile the mixture into the grapefruit shells.

Celery Soup   25 Cals

Metric/Imperial	*American*
225g/8oz celery, chopped	2 cups chopped celery
1 onion, chopped	1 onion, chopped
600ml/1 pint light stock	2½ cups light bouillon
salt	salt
ground black pepper	ground black pepper
½ teaspoon grated nutmeg	½ teaspoon grated nutmeg
25g/1oz skimmed milk powder	2 tablespoons skimmed milk powder
chopped parsley, to garnish	chopped parsley, to garnish

Place the celery, onion, stock, salt, pepper and nutmeg in a pan. Bring to the boil, cover and simmer for 25 minutes. Leave to cool slightly, then place in an electric blender with the skimmed milk powder. Blend until smooth and return to the pan. Bring to the boil, stirring, and cook for 2 minutes. Check the seasoning and pour into hot bowls. Serve sprinkled with parsley.

Sardine and Egg Mousse   105 Cals

Metric/Imperial	*American*
1 x 120g/4¼oz can sardines in tomato juice	1 x 4¼oz can sardines in tomato juice
1 hard-boiled egg, chopped	1 hard-cooked egg, chopped
200ml/⅓ pint natural yogurt	⅞ cup unflavored yogurt
1 teaspoon gelatine	1 teaspoon gelatin
1 teaspoon lemon juice	1 teaspoon lemon juice
salt and pepper	salt and pepper
To garnish:	*To garnish:*
watercress	watercress
egg slices	egg slices

Place the sardines and their juice in a bowl and mash with the egg and yogurt. Place the gelatin(e) in a small bowl with one tablespoon of water and lemon juice and heat over a pan of simmering water until dissolved. Cool and fold into the sardine mixture with salt and pepper. Spoon into 4 ramekin dishes and chill until set. Garnish with watercress and egg slices.

Vegetables and salads

Crunchy Coleslaw   50 Cals

Metric/Imperial
225g/8oz white cabbage,
  finely shredded
2 carrots, grated
1 red dessert apple, cored
  and sliced
2 celery sticks, chopped
2 spring onions, chopped
6 tablespoons natural
  yogurt
1 tablespoon dressing
salt and pepper

American
2 cups shredded white
  cabbage
2 carrots, grated
1 red dessert apple, cored
  and sliced
2 celery stalks, chopped
2 scallions, chopped
6 tablespoons unflavored
  yogurt
1 tablespoon dressing
salt and pepper

Place the cabbage in a bowl and add the next 4 ingredients. Mix together the yogurt, dressing, salt and pepper and add to the salad. Toss well.

Red Cabbage Salad   40 Cals

Metric/Imperial
175g/6oz red cabbage,
  finely shredded
1 small onion, sliced
50g/2oz button
  mushrooms, sliced
5cm/2inch piece
  cucumber, cut into strips
150ml/¼ pint natural
  yogurt
¼ teaspoon caraway seeds
salt and pepper

American
2 cups finely shredded red
  cabbage
1 small onion, sliced
½ cup button mushrooms,
  sliced
2 inch piece cucumber, cut
  into strips
⅔ cup unflavored yogurt
¼ teaspoon caraway seeds
salt and pepper

Place the red cabbage in a bowl and add the onion, mushrooms and cucumber. Mix the yogurt with the caraway seeds, salt and pepper then stir into the vegetables and mix well.

Eastern Cucumber Salad   35 Cals

Metric/Imperial	*American*
1/2 cucumber, cubed	1/2 cucumber, cubed
1 green pepper, cored, seeded and chopped	1 green pepper, cored, seeded and chopped
2 sprigs mint	2 sprigs of mint
150ml/1/4 pint natural yogurt	2/3 cup unflavored yogurt salt and pepper
salt and pepper	

Place the cucumber and green pepper in a bowl. Chop the mint leaves and add with the yogurt and salt and pepper to taste. Serve with curried or hot spicy food.

Low Calorie French Dressing   18 Cals per tablespoon

1 tablespoon olive oil	1/2 teaspoon made mustard
6 tablespoons wine or cider vinegar	salt and pepper
3 drops of liquid sweetener	1/4 teaspoon mixed herbs (optional)

Place all the ingredients in a screw-top jar and shake vigorously until well blended.

Vegetable à Provence   60 Cals

Metric/Imperial	*American*
7g/1/4oz margarine	2 tablespoons margarine
1 onion, chopped	1 onion, chopped
2 cloves garlic, crushed	2 cloves garlic, crushed
2 green peppers, cored, seeded and sliced	2 green peppers, cored, seeded and sliced
225g/8oz courgettes, sliced	1/2lb zucchini, sliced
1 × 400g/14oz can tomatoes, drained	1 × 14oz can tomatoes, drained
1 teaspoon mixed herbs	1 teaspoon mixed herbs
salt and pepper	salt and pepper

Melt the margarine in a pan and fry the onion and garlic until soft. Add all remaining ingredients. Bring to the boil, cover and simmer for 15 to 20 minutes. Serve hot or cold.

Vegetarian dishes

Vegetable Hotpot   180 Cals

Metric/Imperial

225g/8oz swede, sliced
2 carrots, sliced
1 onion, sliced
2 celery sticks, chopped
100g/4oz frozen peas
1 × 225g/8oz can baked
  beans
50g/2oz peanuts, chopped
salt and pepper
1 × 400g/14oz can
  tomatoes
chopped parsley, to garnish

American

1 1/2 cups sliced swede
2 carrots, sliced
1 onion, sliced
2 celery stalks, chopped
3/4 cup frozen peas
1 × 8oz can baked beans
1/2 cup chopped peanuts
salt and pepper
1 × 14oz can tomatoes
chopped parsley, to garnish

Grease a 1.75 litre/3 pint/7 1/2 cup casserole. Arrange the vegetables, beans and nuts in layers, sprinkling each with salt and pepper. Pour the tomatoes and their juice over the top, cover and cook in a moderate oven (180°C/350°F, Gas Mark 4) for 1 to 1 1/4 hours. Serve hot, garnished with parsley.

Stuffed Peppers   180 Cals

Metric/Imperial

4 medium green peppers
salt and pepper
75g/3oz brown rice
1 small onion, chopped
100g/4oz cottage cheese
50g/2oz Edam cheese,
  grated
2 tomatoes, chopped
1 tablespoon parsley
1/2 teaspoon made mustard
salt and pepper

American

4 medium green peppers
salt and pepper
1/2 cup brown rice
1 small onion, chopped
1/2 cup cottage cheese
1/2 cup grated Edam cheese
2 tomatoes, chopped
1 tablespoon parsley
1/2 teaspoon made mustard
salt and pepper

Cut the tops from the peppers and reserve; discard the seeds and cores. Blanch in boiling salted water for 2 minutes, remove and drain. Cook the rice in boiling salted water until soft. Drain and rinse thoroughly. Place the rice in a bowl and add the remaining ingredients. Mix well and add salt and pepper to taste. Pile the mixture into the pepper shells and replace the tops. Place in a greased shallow ovenproof dish, cover with foil and cook in a moderate oven (180°C/350°F, Gas Mark 4) for 15 to 20 minutes. Serve hot.

Vegetarian Rissoles

300 Cals: 150 Cals per rissole

Metric/Imperial	American
225g/8oz lentils	1 cup lentils
40g/1½oz low-Calorie spread	3 tablespoons low-Calorie spread
1 onion, chopped	1 onion, finely chopped
2 celery sticks, chopped	2 celery stalks, chopped
50g/2oz Edam cheese, grated	½ cup grated Edam cheese
50g/2oz low-Calorie breadcrumbs	1 cup low-Calorie breadcrumbs
2 tablespoons parsley	2 tablespoons parsley
garlic granules	garlic granules
salt and pepper	salt and pepper
2 teaspoons mixed herbs	2 teaspoons mixed herbs
1 egg, beaten	1 egg, beaten

Soak the lentils in cold water for a few hours then place in a pan and cover with fresh cold water. Bring to the boil and cook for 30 minutes. Drain thoroughly. Melt one third of the low-Calorie spread in a frying pan (skillet) and fry the onion and celery until soft. Mix with the lentils and all other ingredients. Shape into 8 rissoles. Melt the remaining low-Calorie spread in a pan and cook the rissoles for 6 to 8 minutes, turning once. Remove with a slotted spoon and place on kitchen paper (towels) to absorb excess fat.

75

Savoury Spinach Bake   190 Cals

Metric/Imperial	American
500g/1lb frozen spinach, thawed	2 cups thawed frozen spinach
350g/12oz cottage cheese	1½ cups cottage cheese
salt, pepper, grated nutmeg	salt, pepper, grated nutmeg
25g/1oz walnuts, chopped	¼ cup chopped walnuts
1 hard-boiled egg, chopped	1 hard-cooked egg, chopped
tomato slices, to garnish	tomato slices, to garnish

Cook the spinach as directed on the packet and drain. Combine with the cottage cheese, salt and pepper, nutmeg, walnuts and egg. Mix well and divide between 4 small greased ovenproof dishes. Place in a moderate oven (160°C/325°F, Gas Mark 3) for 20 minutes. Serve garnished with the tomato.

Egg and Bean Savoury   185 Cals

Metric/Imperial	American
4 hard-boiled eggs, shelled and kept warm	4 hard-cooked eggs, shelled and kept warm
7g/¼oz margarine	2 teaspoons margarine
1 small onion, chopped	1 small onion, chopped
3 teaspoons tomato purée	3 teaspoons tomato paste
1 drop liquid sweetener	1 drop liquid sweetener
150ml/¼ pint natural yogurt	⅔ cup unflavored yogurt
1 × 225g/8oz can red kidney beans, drained	1 × 8oz can red kidney beans, drained
salt and pepper	salt and pepper
chopped parsley, to garnish	chopped parsley, to garnish

Cut the eggs in half and arrange in a shallow serving dish. Melt the margarine in a pan and fry the onion until soft. Add the tomato purée (paste) and cook for 2 minutes, then stir in the sweetener, yogurt, kidney beans and salt and pepper to taste. Heat gently then pour the bean mixture over the eggs. Garnish with parsley and serve immediately.

Cottage Cheese and Nut Platter   225 Cals

Metric/Imperial	*American*
a few lettuce leaves, washed and drained	a few lettuce leaves, washed and drained
2 dessert apples, cored and sliced	2 dessert apples, cored and sliced
2 teaspoons lemon juice	2 teaspoons lemon juice
225g/8oz grapes, halved	2 cups grapes, halved
500g/1lb cottage cheese	2 cups cottage cheese
50g/2oz hazelnuts, crushed	1/3 cup crushed filberts
salt and pepper	salt and pepper

Arrange the lettuce leaves on a serving plate. Toss the apple slices in the lemon juice and arrange inside the lettuce with the grapes.

Place the cottage cheese in a bowl with half the hazelnuts (filberts). Add salt and pepper to taste. Pile the mixture into the centre of the plate. Arrange the remaining hazelnuts (filberts) on top.

Farmhouse Omelet   250 Cals

Metric/Imperial	*American*
50g/2oz low-Calorie spread	1/4 cup low-Calorie spread
1 large onion, chopped	1 large onion, chopped
1 red pepper, cored, seeded and chopped	1 red pepper, cored, seeded and chopped
50g/2oz mushrooms, sliced	1/2 cup sliced mushrooms
100g/4oz frozen mixed vegetables, cooked	3/4 cup frozen mixed vegetables, cooked
6 eggs	6 eggs
salt and pepper	salt and pepper
2 teaspoons mixed herbs	2 teaspoons mixed herbs
watercress, to garnish	watercress, to garnish

Melt the low-Calorie spread in a large frying pan (skillet) and fry the onion, pepper and mushrooms until soft. Stir in the mixed vegetables. Beat together the eggs, salt, pepper and herbs with 1 tablespoon of water. Add to the pan and cook over a moderate heat until the mixture sets underneath. Continue cooking for 1 minute, then place under a moderate grill to set the top. Garnish with watercress.

Meat and fish dishes

Pork and Orange Kebabs 360 Cals, 375 Cals with sauce

Metric/Imperial

500g/1lb pork fillet, cut
  into small cubes
2 oranges, segmented
1 green pepper, seeded and
  cut into 2.5cm/1 inch
  pieces
2 celery sticks, cut into
  2.5cm/1 inch pieces
salt and pepper
1 tablespoon oil
Sauce:
2 teaspoons cornflour
150ml/¼ pint orange juice
150ml/¼ pint stock
salt and pepper

American

1lb pork tenderloin, cut into
  small cubes
2 oranges, segmented
1 green pepper, seeded and
  cut into 1 inch pieces
2 celery stalks, cut into 1
  inch pieces
salt and pepper
1 tablespoon oil
Sauce:
2 teaspoons cornstarch
⅔ cup orange juice
⅔ cup bouillon
salt and pepper

Thread the first 4 ingredients on to 4 skewers. Sprinkle with
salt and pepper and brush lightly with oil. Cook under a
moderate grill for 20 minutes, turning occasionally. To
make the sauce, blend the cornflour (cornstarch) with a
little cold orange juice and stir in the remaining juice and
stock (bouillon). Add salt and pepper to taste and heat,
stirring until the sauce thickens. Continue to cook for 1
minute. Serve separately with the kebabs.

Turkey Curry   185 Cals curry only

Metric/Imperial   *American*

1 tablespoon oil	1 tablespoon oil
2 cloves, crushed	2 cloves, crushed
½ teaspoon ground ginger	½ teaspoon ground ginger
1½ teaspoon ground coriander	1½ teaspoons ground coriander
1 teaspoon ground turmeric	1 teaspoon ground turmeric
1 teaspoon cumin seeds	1 teaspoon cumin seeds
½ teaspoon chilli powder	½ teaspoon chilli powder
3 cloves garlic, crushed	3 cloves garlic, crushed
2 onions, sliced	2 onions, sliced
1 × 400g/14oz can tomatoes	1 × 14oz can tomatoes
150ml/¼ pint stock	⅔ cup bouillon
salt and pepper	salt and pepper
350g/12oz cooked turkey meat, chopped	1½ cups chopped cooked turkey meat

Heat the oil in a pan and add the next 6 ingredients. Fry the spices for 2 minutes then add the garlic and onions. Cook for 1 minute then add the tomatoes with their juice, stock and salt and pepper to taste. Bring to the boil, cover and simmer for 30 minutes. Add the turkey meat and cook for 1 hour until the sauce is reduced to a thick gravy. Serve with boiled rice, natural (unflavored) yogurt, sliced cucumber and tomatoes.

Orange and Lemon Chicken   215 Cals

Metric/Imperial/American

4 chicken joints, skinned	1 clove garlic, crushed
1 tablespoon oil	½ teaspoon ground ginger
rind and juice of 1 lemon	salt and pepper
rind and juice of 1 orange	watercress, to garnish

Place the chicken joints in a greased, shallow ovenproof dish. Mix together the oil, lemon and orange rinds and juice, garlic, ginger, salt and pepper. Pour over the chicken and cover with foil. Place in a moderately hot oven (190°C/375°F, Gas Mark 5) for 1 hour. Remove the foil and continue to cook for 15 to 20 minutes. Serve garnished with watercress.

Kidneys in Lemon Sauce   140 Cals

Metric/Imperial

15g/½oz low-Calorie
  spread
1 small onion, chopped
1 celery stick, chopped
8 lambs' kidneys, skin
  removed and cored
15g/½oz plain flour
rind and juice of ½ lemon
200ml/⅓ pint stock
salt and pepper
1 teaspoon dried thyme
chopped parsley, to garnish

American

1 tablespoon low-Calorie
  spread
1 small onion, chopped
1 celery stalk, chopped
8 lambs' kidneys, skin
  removed and cored
2 tablespoons all-purpose
  flour
rind and juice of ½ lemon
⅞ cup bouillon
salt and pepper
1 teaspoon dried thyme
chopped parsley, to garnish

Melt the low-Calorie spread in a pan and fry the onion and
celery until soft. Coat the halved kidneys in flour and fry in
the pan until browned all over. Add the remaining ingredients except the parsley. Heat, stirring until the mixture
comes to the boil. Cover and simmer for 20 to 25 minutes.
Garnish with parsley.

Barbecued Liver   250 Cals

Metric/Imperial

1 tablespoon oil
1 large onion, chopped
1 celery stick, chopped
½ green pepper, cored,
  seeded and chopped
2 teaspoons made mustard
1 teaspoon paprika
salt and pepper
1 tablespoon tomato purée
1 tablespoon
  Worcestershire sauce
1 tablespoon vinegar
6 drops liquid sweetener
200ml/⅓ pint stock
500g/1lb lambs' liver
chopped parsley, to garnish

American

1 tablespoon oil
1 large onion, chopped
1 celery stalk, chopped
½ green pepper, cored,
  seeded and chopped
2 teaspoons made mustard
1 teaspoon paprika
salt and pepper
1 tablespoon tomato paste
1 tablespoon
  Worcestershire sauce
1 tablespoon vinegar
6 drops liquid sweetener
⅞ cup bouillon
1lb lambs' liver
chopped parsley, to garnish

Heat the oil in a frying pan (skillet) and fry the onion, celery and pepper until soft. Stir in the mustard, paprika, salt and pepper and continue to cook for 1 minute. Add the tomato purée (paste), Worcestershire sauce, vinegar, sweetener and stock (bouillon). Bring to the boil, cover and simmer for 15 minutes. Remove the veins from the liver, slice and arrange in a shallow ovenproof dish. Pour the sauce over. Cover with aluminium foil and place in a moderate oven (180°C/350°F, Gas Mark 4) for 1 hour. Serve garnished with parsley.

Chicken Parcels   225 Cals

Metric/Imperial	American
4 chicken joints, skinned	4 chicken joints, skinned
1 clove garlic, crushed	1 clove garlic, crushed
salt and pepper	salt and pepper
1 onion, sliced	1 onion, sliced
1 green pepper, cored, seeded and chopped	1 green pepper, cored, seeded and chopped
1 teaspoon vinegar	1 teaspoon vinegar
3 teaspoons soy sauce	3 teaspoons soy sauce
1/2 teaspoon made mustard	1/2 teaspoon made mustard
3 drops liquid sweetener	3 drops liquid sweetener
2 pineapple rings, chopped	2 pineapple rings, chopped
120ml/4fl oz stock	1/2 cup bouillon
1 teaspoon cornflour	1 teaspoon cornstarch
watercress, to garnish	watercress, to garnish

Place each chicken piece on a piece of aluminium foil. Rub over with garlic, salt and pepper. Place the onion in a saucepan with the next 7 ingredients. Bring to the boil, cover and simmer for 5 to 10 minutes. Blend the cornflour (cornstarch) with a little cold water and add to the pan. Continue to cook for 1 minute, then check the seasoning. Divide the mixture between the chicken pieces and wrap the foil over. Place the parcels on a baking sheet and cook in a moderate oven (180°C/350°F, Gas Mark 4) for 1 hour. Remove the foil and serve garnished with watercress.

Mushroom and Yogurt Topped lamb 250 Cals

Metric/Imperial	American
4 lamb chops	4 lamb chops
75g/3oz mushrooms, sliced	1 cup sliced mushrooms
150ml/¼ pint natural yogurt	⅔ cup unflavored yogurt
2 teaspoons tomato purée	2 teaspoons tomato paste
½ teaspoon sugar	½ teaspoon sugar
2 teaspoons paprika	2 teaspoons paprika
parsley, to garnish	parsley, to garnish
Marinade:	Marinade:
2 tablespoons white wine	2 tablespoons white wine
2 teaspoons lemon juice	2 teaspoons lemon juice
½ teaspoon dried thyme	½ teaspoon dried thyme
salt and pepper	salt and pepper

Mix together the marinade ingredients. Trim the chops, removing any excess fat and place in the marinade for 2 to 3 hours. Drain the chops and dry with kitchen paper (towels). Place them in a shallow ovenproof dish. Arrange the mushrooms over the top and cover with foil. Cook in a moderately hot oven (190°C/375°F, Gas Mark 5) for 1 hour. Mix together the yogurt, tomato purée (paste), sugar and paprika and spoon over the chops. Continue cooking for 15 minutes. Serve garnished with parsley.

Sweet and Sour Cod Steaks 125 Cals

Metric/Imperial	American
4 cod steaks	4 cod steaks
salt and pepper	salt and pepper
1 onion, sliced	1 onion, sliced
1 green pepper, cored, seeded and chopped	1 green pepper, cored, seeded and chopped
1 × 225g/8oz can pineapple pieces, drained	1 × 8oz can pineapple pieces, drained
1 × 225g/8oz can tomatoes	1 × 8oz can tomatoes
1 tablespoon vinegar	1 tablespoon vinegar
1 tablespoon soy sauce	1 tablespoon soy sauce
4 tablespoons water	4 tablespoons water
liquid sweetener, to taste	liquid sweetener, to taste

Place the cod steaks in a shallow ovenproof dish and sprinkle with salt and pepper. Place the remaining ingredients in a pan and add salt and pepper to taste. Bring to the boil, stirring, cover and simmer for 15 to 20 minutes. Pour over the fish, cover with aluminium foil and place in a moderately hot oven (190°C/375°F, Gas Mark 5) for 25 to 30 minutes until the fish is cooked. Serve with green vegetables.

Tomato Smoked Haddock — 175 Cals

Metric/Imperial	American
4 spring onions, chopped	4 scallions, chopped
3 tomatoes, chopped	3 tomatoes, chopped
100g/4oz frozen mixed vegetables, cooked	¾ cup cooked frozen mixed vegetables
salt and pepper	salt and pepper
½ teaspoon oregano	½ teaspoon oregano
500g/1lb smoked haddock fillet	1lb smoked haddock fillet
15g/½oz butter	1 tablespoon butter
150ml/¼ pint tomato juice	⅔ cup tomato juice
parsley, to garnish	parsley, to garnish

Mix together the spring onions (scallions), tomatoes, mixed vegetables, salt, pepper and oregano then place in a shallow, ovenproof dish. Cut the haddock into 4 portions and arrange over the vegetables. Dot with the butter and pour on the tomato juice. Cover with aluminium foil and cook in a moderately hot oven (190°C/350°F, Gas Mark 5) for 30 minutes. Serve garnished with parsley.

Rolled Plaice (Flounder) Provençal   210 Cals

Metric/Imperial	*American*
4 plaice fillets	4 flounder fillets
25g/1oz low-Calorie spread	2 tablespoons low-Calorie spread
1 onion, finely chopped	1 onion, finely chopped
1 clove garlic, crushed	1 clove garlic, crushed
50g/2oz mushrooms, sliced	½ cup sliced mushrooms
25g/1oz plain flour	¼ cup all-purpose flour
2 tablespoons tomato purée	2 tablespoons tomato paste
150ml/¼ pint white wine	⅔ cup white wine
150ml/¼ pint light stock	⅔ cup bouillon
1 tablespoon parsley	1 tablespoon parsley
salt and pepper	salt and pepper
liquid sweetener, to taste	liquid sweetener to taste

Roll the plaice (flounder) fillets and arrange in a shallow ovenproof dish. Melt the low-Calorie spread in a pan and lightly fry the onion, garlic and mushrooms. Stir in the flour and cook for 1 minute. Remove from the heat and stir in the tomato purée (paste), wine, stock and parsley. Heat, stirring until the sauce thickens. Add salt, pepper and sweetener to taste and continue cooking for 1 minute. Pour the sauce over the fish, cover with aluminium foil and place in a moderate oven (180°C/350°F, Gas Mark 4) for 20 to 30 minutes.

Tuna and Egg Bake   190 Cals

Metric/Imperial	*American*
1 × 200g/7oz can tuna, drained and flaked	1 × 7oz can tuna, drained and flaked
black pepper	black pepper
4 hard-boiled eggs, sliced	4 hard-cooked eggs, sliced
150ml/¼ pint tomato juice	⅔ cup tomato juice
4 tomatoes, sliced	4 tomatoes, sliced
salt and pepper	salt and pepper
50g/2oz low-Calorie breadcrumbs	1 cup low-Calorie breadcrumbs
1 teaspoon mixed herbs	1 teaspoon mixed herbs

Place the tuna in a 1.2 litre/2 pint/5 cup ovenproof dish and sprinkle with pepper. Arrange the eggs on top and pour the tomato juice over. Arrange the tomato slices over and sprinkle with salt and pepper. Mix together the breadcrumbs and herbs and spoon over the tomatoes. Place in a moderate oven (180°C/350°F, Gas Mark 4) for 20 minutes. Serve with green salad.

Desserts

Plums with Meringue Topping   125 Cals

Metric/Imperial	American
500g/1lb plums, halved and stoned	1lb plums, halved and stoned
liquid sweetener, to taste	liquid sweetener, to taste
2 egg whites	2 egg whites
75g/3oz caster sugar	6 tablespoons sugar

Wash the plums and place in a pan with 1 tablespoon of water. Cook gently until the fruit is soft, then add sweetener to taste. Spoon into a 900ml/1½ pint/3¾ cup ovenproof dish. Whisk the egg whites until stiff, then whisk in half the sugar. Fold in the remaining sugar with a metal spoon and pile or pipe over the plums. Place in a moderate oven (180°C/350°F, Gas Mark 4) for 15 minutes or until the meringue is just turning brown. Serve hot or cold.

Grape Brûlée   115 Cals

Metric/Imperial	American
225g/8oz green grapes	2 cups white grapes
150ml/¼ pint sour cream	⅔ cup sour cream
25g/1oz soft brown sugar	¼ cup soft brown sugar
1 tablespoon chopped nuts	1 tablespoon chopped nuts

Cut the grapes in half and remove the pips (seeds). Divide between 4 individual heatproof dishes. Spoon the cream over and chill well. Before serving sprinkle with sugar and nuts and place under a hot grill for 1 to 2 minutes. Serve immediately.

Blackcurrant Fluff   85 Cals

Metric/Imperial	American
350g/12oz blackcurrants	3 cups blackcurrants
liquid sweetener, to taste	liquid sweetener, to taste
150ml/¼ pint natural yogurt	⅔ cup unflavored yogurt
150ml/¼ pint blackcurrant yogurt	⅔ cup blackcurrant yogurt
2 egg whites	2 egg whites
blackcurrants, to decorate	blackcurrants, to decorate

Trim and wash the blackcurrants; place in a pan with 1 tablespoon of water. Cook gently until the fruit is soft. Add sweetener to taste and leave to cool. Place the fruit in an electric blender or pass through a sieve (strainer) to make a purée. Mix together the natural (unflavored) and blackcurrant yogurt and add the purée. Mix well. Whisk the egg whites until stiff and fold into the fruit mixture. Spoon into 4 sundae dishes and decorate with blackcurrants. Serve chilled.

Sultana Baked Apples   95 Cals, 125 Cals with cream

Metric/Imperial	American
4 x 150g/5oz cooking apples	4 x 5oz cooking apples
2 tablespoons sultanas	2 tablespoons seedless white raisins
1 tablespoon soft brown sugar	1 tablespoon soft brown sugar
150ml/¼ pint orange juice	⅔ cup orange juice
4 tablespoons single cream (optional)	¼ cup light cream (optional)

Remove the core from the apples and score the skins around the middle. Fill the centres with the sultanas (seedless white raisins) and sugar. Place in a shallow overproof dish and pour the orange juice over. Cook in a moderately hot oven (190°C/375°F, Gas Mark 5) for 30 minutes. Serve hot or cold with the cream, if using.

Baked Bananas with Orange   100 Cals,
125 Cals with cream

Metric/Imperial/American

4 bananas, thickly sliced	2 teaspoons honey
2 teaspoons lemon juice	4 tablespoons sour cream
rind and juice of 1 orange	

Place the bananas in an ovenproof dish and sprinkle with the lemon juice. Toss well. Blend the grated orange rind, juice and honey together and pour over the bananas. Cover with foil and cook in a moderate oven (180°C/350°F, Gas Mark 4) for 20 minutes. Serve hot with cream.

Apricot Fool   50 Cals

Metric/Imperial	*American*
350g/12oz apricots, halved and stone removed	¾lb apricots, halved and seed removed
liquid sweetener, to taste	liquid sweetener, to taste
1 tablespoon custard powder	1 tablespoon custard powder
300ml/½ pint skimmed milk	1¼ cups skimmed milk
apricot slices, to decorate	apricot slices, to decorate

Place the apricots in a pan with 2 tablespoons of water and cook gently until the fruit is soft. Add sweetener to taste and leave to cool. Place the fruit in an electric blender or sieve (strain) to make a purée. Blend the custard powder with a little of the milk. Heat the remaining milk and stir into the custard mixture, then return to the pan. Heat, stirring continuously until the custard thickens. Cook for 1 minute. Add sweetener to taste and leave to cool. Whisk together the fruit purée and custard until well blended. Spoon into 4 dishes and decorate with the apricot slices. Chill before serving.

Blackberry Sorbet
70 Cals

Metric/Imperial	*American*
225g/8oz fresh or frozen blackberries	1⅔ cups fresh or frozen blackberries
300ml/½ pint natural yogurt	1¼ cups unflavored yogurt
2 teaspoons gelatine	2 teaspoons gelatin
2 teaspoons lemon juice	2 teaspoons lemon juice
liquid sweetener, to taste	liquid sweetener to taste
2 egg whites	2 egg whites

Sieve (strain) the blackberries to make a purée and remove the seeds, then combine with yogurt. Dissolve the gelatin(e) in 2 tablespoons of water and lemon juice over a pan of gently simmering water. Cool and stir into the fruit mixture with sweetener to taste. Whisk the egg whites until stiff and fold into the blackberry mixture. Pour into a shallow container and freeze. Before serving transfer to the refrigerator for about 30 minutes. Spoon into sundae dishes.

Coeur à la Crème
125 Cals

Metric/Imperial	*American*
350g/12oz cottage cheese, sieved	1½ cups cottage cheese, sieved
150ml/¼ pint natural yogurt	⅔ cup unflavored yogurt
2 teaspoons gelatine	2 teaspoons gelatin
juice of ½ lemon	juice of ½ lemon
liquid sweetener, to taste	liquid sweetener, to taste
225g/8oz fresh or frozen raspberries	1⅔ cups fresh or frozen raspberries

Mix together the cottage cheese and yogurt. Dissolve the gelatin(e) in 2 tablespoons of water and lemon juice over a pan of gently simmering water. Cool and fold into the cheese mixture with sweetener to taste. Spoon into 4 individual moulds (molds) and leave in the refrigerator overnight to set. Serve in the dishes or turn out and decorate with the raspberries.

Calorie charts

Food values, unless otherwise stated are for 1 oz (25 g) by weight.

A

1 oz almonds	170
1 oz apples, raw	
dessert and cooking	10
1 tablespoon apple	
sauce	25
1 oz apricots, fresh	5
dried raw	50
tinned in syrup	30
1 teaspoon arrowroot	10
1 oz artichoke, globe	5
jerusalem	5
1 oz aubergine, raw	5
fried,	60
1 oz avocado pear	
(without stone)	65

B

1 oz bacon, back fried	130
back grilled	115
back raw	120
streaky fried	140
streaky grilled	120
streaky raw	115
1 oz banana flesh	20
1 oz pearl barley, raw	100
boiled	35
1 oz beans, baked in	
tomato sauce	25
broad, fresh	10
boiled	15
haricot, dried	75
kidney, canned,	
drained	25
lima, fresh	10
navy, dried	75
runner, boiled	5

soya, raw	115
1 oz bean sprouts, raw	10
1 oz beef, lean, rump	
uncooked	55
corned	60
minced, uncooked	65
cooked	45
steak, grilled	55
topside, lean, roast	45
1 oz biscuits, plain	125
sweet	160
1 oz blackberries	10
1 oz blackcurrants	10
1 oz brazil nuts	185
1 oz bread, white or	
brown	70
wholemeal	65
1 slice low-calorie bread	40
1 oz breakfast cereal	100
1 oz broccoli, boiled	5
1 oz brussels sprouts,	
boiled	5
1 oz butter	225

C

1 oz cabbage, boiled	5
1 oz cake, plain fruit	105
rich fruit	110
sponge	85
1 oz carrots, boiled	5
1 oz cauliflower, boiled	5
1 oz celery	neg
1 oz cheese, brie	90
caerphilly	120
camembert	90
cheddar	120
cottage	30

cream	130
curd	40
danish blue	105
double gloucester	105
edam	90
gorgonzola	110
gouda	95
parmesan	120
processed	105
stilton, blue	120
1 oz cherries, with stone	10
1 oz chicken meat,	
uncooked	35
roasted	40
1 oz chocolate, milk,	165
plain	155
1 teaspoon cocoa	
powder	5
1 oz dessicated	
coconut	170
1 oz cod, fillet	20
steamed	25
1 oz cod roe	35
1 oz cornflakes	100
1 oz cornflour	100
1 oz corn oil	260
1 oz corn on the cob,	
kernels only	35
1 oz courgettes	3
1 oz cream, clotted	165
double (heavy)	125
single	60
sour	55
whipping	95
1 oz cucumber	3
1 oz currants, dried	70
1 teaspoon curry powder	10
1 oz custard powder	100

D

1 oz dates, dried with	
stones	60

1 oz duck, meat only	
roasted	55

E

2 oz egg, raw, boiled	90
yolk	60
white	15
1 oz eggplant	5

F

1 oz figs, dried	60
1 oz filberts, shelled	110
1 oz flounder	15
1 oz flour, white	100
wholemeal	95

G

1 clove garlic	neg
1 tablespoon gelatine	30
1 oz gherkins	5
1 oz goose, meat only	
roast	90
1 oz gooseberries	10
1 oz grapefruit, flesh	5
whole fruit	3
juice	10
1 oz grapes,	15

H

1 oz haddock, smoked	
or unsmoked	20
raw on bone	15
1 oz hake, steamed on	
bone	25
1 oz halibut, steamed	
on bone	30
1 oz ham, lean, boiled	35
chopped, canned	75
1 oz hazelnuts, shelled	110
1 oz herring, grilled on	
bone	40
fillet, grilled	55

1 oz honey	80
1 tablespoon horseradish sauce	15

I

1 oz ice cream	50

J

1 oz jam	75

K

1 oz kidney	25
1 oz kippers, raw	30
baked or grilled	60

L

1 oz lamb, lean	
uncooked	45
leg roast	75
shoulder roast	90
1 oz lard (shortening)	260
1 oz leeks	10
1 oz lemon, with peel	4
1 oz lemon curd	85
1 oz lemon sole	
fillet, grilled or steamed	25
1 oz lentils, raw	85
boiled	30
1 oz lettuce	5
1 oz liver, raw	
chicken	40
lamb	50
pig's	45
1 oz low-fat spread	105
1 oz luncheon meat	90

M

1 oz macaroni, raw	100
boiled	35
1 oz mackerel, raw	30
fillet fried	55

1 oz mandarin oranges,	
fresh with peel	5
canned, drained	15
1 oz margarine	215
1 oz marmalade	75
1 oz marrow, boiled	neg
1 oz melon	5
1 pint milk	370
skimmed	200
evaporated, 1 tablespoon	25
1 oz mincemeat	75
1 oz muesli	105
1 oz mushrooms	
uncooked	2
fried	60
1 teaspoon made mustard	10

N

1 oz nectarines, with peel	15
1 oz noodles, cooked	35

O

1 oz oats, porridge	115
1 oz olive oil	265
1 oz olives, with stones	25
1 oz onions, raw	5
fried	100
spring	10
1 oz oranges, flesh	10
with peel,	5
juice	10
1 oz oysters, shelled	15

P

1 oz parsley, fresh	5
1 oz parsnip, raw	15
boiled	15
roast	30
1 oz pastry, flaky baked	165

shortcrust baked	155	roast, small	50
1 oz peaches, with		sauté	50
stones	10	instant powder	105
canned in syrup	25	1 oz prawns, shelled	30
1 oz peanuts, shelled,		1 oz prunes, dried	40
roasted, salted	160	stewed without sugar	25
butter	175	juice	25
1 oz pears, fresh	10	1 oz pumpkin, raw	5
canned in syrup	20		
1 oz peas, fresh or frozen	20	**R**	
canned, processed	25	1 oz radishes	4
dried, boiled	30	1 oz raisins	70
split, boiled	35	1 oz raspberries, fresh	5
chick, raw	90	canned, drained	25
1 pecan nut	15	1 oz redcurrants	5
1 oz peppers, red or		1 oz rhubarb, stewed	neg
green, raw	10	1 oz rice, raw	100
1 oz pickle, sweet	40	boiled	35
1 oz pilchards, canned			
in sauce	35	**S**	
1 oz pineapple, fresh	15	1 oz salad cream	90-120
canned in syrup	20	1 oz salmon, on bone	
1 oz plaice, with		uncooked	50
bones, raw	15	tinned	40
fillet, steamed	25	smoked	40
1 oz plums, fresh with		steamed, fillet	55
stones	10	1 oz sardines, canned	
stewed with no sugar	5	drained	60
canned in syrup	20	1 oz salt	neg
1 oz pork, lean,		1 oz sausage, beef	
uncooked	40	fried or grilled	75
roast	50	pork, fried or grilled	95
crackling	190	1 oz scampi, fried in	
scratchings	185	batter	85
4 oz pork chop, grilled	290	1 oz semolina, raw	100
1 oz potatoes, raw	25	1 oz shrimps, whole,	
boiled, old	25	boiled	10
boiled, new	20	without shells,	35
chips, average size	70	jumbo, fried in batter	85
crisps	150	1 oz sole, raw on bone	15
roast, large	40	fillet, steamed	25
roast, medium	45	fillet, fried	60

1 tablespoon soy sauce	5
1 oz spaghetti, raw	105
canned in tomato sauce	20
boiled	35
1 oz spinach, boiled	10
1 oz spring greens, boiled	5
1 oz strawberries, fresh	5
canned in syrup, drained	25
1 stock cube	20-30
1 oz suet, shredded	235
1 oz sugar, white or brown caster, demerara etc	110
1 oz sultanas	70
1 oz sunflower seeds	170
1 oz sunflower seed oil	255
1 oz swedes, raw	5
boiled	5
1 oz sweetcorn, canned	20
frozen	25
1 oz sweets, boiled	95-110
fruit gums	55-95
fudge	125-130
toffees	110-130
peppermints	110
1 oz syrup, golden	85
maple	70
rosehip	65

T

1 oz tangerine, flesh	10
with peel	5
1 oz tomatoes, raw or grilled	5
canned	5
purée, concentrated (paste)	30
ketchup (catsup)	30
1 oz trout, steamed on bone	25

1 oz tuna, canned	85
drained	60
1 oz turkey, meat only	
raw	30
roast	40
1 oz turnips, raw	5

V

1 oz veal fillet, raw	30
roast	65
fried in breadcrumbs	60
1 oz vinegar	neg

W

1 oz walnuts	155
1 oz watercress	5
1 oz watermelon	5
1 oz wheatgerm	100
1 oz whiting, fillet raw	15
steamed	20
1 oz Worcestershire sauce	20

Y

1 oz yams, cooked	35
1 oz yogurt, plain, low fat	15
fruit, low fat	25

Z

1 oz zucchini	3

CALORIE CHARTS

Calorie values for alcoholic drinks and soft drinks.

These are average figures as varying brands may differ slightly.

Beer (Calories per 300ml/½ pint/1¼ cups)

Brown ale	80
Draught bitter	90
Draught mild	70
Bottled stout	100
Pale ale	90
Lager	75

Cider (Calories per 300ml/½ pint/1¼ cups)

Dry cider	95
Sweet cider	140
Dry pomagne (sparkling cider)	140
Sweet pomagne	190

Liqueurs (Calories per 1 fl oz/25ml, average measure little less)

Brandy	80
Benedictine	110
Cointreau	100
Crème de menthe	95
Tia Maria	90

Spirits (Calories per 1 fl oz/ 25ml, average measure little less)

Whisky	60
Gin	60
Rum	60
Vodka	60

Values given for 70° proof.
At 80° proof = 70 Calories;
at 90° proof = 80 Calories.

Soft drinks (1 fl oz = 25ml)

1 fl oz blackcurrant health drink, undiluted	60
1 fl oz bitter lemon	15
1 fl oz coca cola	15
1 fl oz fanta orange	15
1 fl oz ginger ale	10
1 fl oz lemonade	10
1 fl oz soda water	neg
1 fl oz tonic water	10

Wine (Calories per 115ml/4 fl oz wineglass)

Dry white	80
Sparkling white	90
Sweet white	100
Dry red	80
Sweet red	95
Rosé	90

Sherry and Vermouth (Calories per 50 ml/2 fl oz measure)

Dry sherry	60
Medium sherry	70
Sweet sherry	80
Dry vermouth	60
Sweet vermouth	70
Campari	120
Port	75

General index

Recipe index

PDO 81-690